Ageless WISDOM

Ageless WISDOM

LIFETIME LESSONS FROM THE BIBLE

Christopher M. Bellitto

Holly
Share your wisdom —
Peace,
[signature]

Paulist Press
New York / Mahwah, NJ

Cover stained glass image by Cain - White Architectural Art Glass
Cover and book design by Lynn Else

Library of Congress Cataloging-in-Publication Data

Names: Bellitto, Christopher M., author.
Title: Ageless wisdom : lifetime lessons from the Bible / Christopher M. Bellitto.
Description: New York : Paulist Press, 2016. | Includes bibliographical references.
Identifiers: LCCN 2015042163 (print) | LCCN 2016001204 (ebook) | ISBN
    9780809149902 (pbk. : alk. paper) | ISBN 9781587686177 (Ebook)
Subjects: LCSH: Wisdom—Biblical teaching. | Aging—Biblical teaching. | Bible—
    Criticism, interpretation, etc.
Classification: LCC BV4650 .B45 2016 (print) | LCC BV4650 (ebook) | DDC
    248.8/5—dc23
LC record available at http://lccn.loc.gov/2015042163

ISBN 978-0-8091-4990-2 (paperback)
ISBN 978-1-58768-617-7 (e-book)

Published by Paulist Press
997 Macarthur Boulevard
Mahwah, New Jersey 07430

www.paulistpress.com

Printed and bound in the
United States of America

To our daughter, Grace,
a wise soul

Contents

Contents

Acknowledgments

I first thought of this book idea more than a decade ago, but other projects, life events, and career paths intervened, which turned out to be for the best: it's the kind of project that needed time and passing years (including my own) to percolate. Many people have helped me on this journey, and it is a pleasure to thank them for their guidance, suggestions, and corrections: Enrique Aguilar, Colt Anderson, Rev. Peter Antoci, Anthony Bellitto, the late Rev. Larry Boadt, CSP, the late Larry Bond, the late Ray Bulman and the members of Columbia University's Studies in Religion Seminar, the late Rev. Francis Corry, Kevin di Camillo (who was a kind of godfather to this manuscript all the way along), Ed and Joanne Dobransky, Zach Flanagin, David Gibson, Bríd Nicholson, Sue Gronewold, Beth Hyde, Tom Izbicki, Xurong Kong, Ian Levy, James Martin, SJ, Elena Procario-Foley, Jack Renard, and Rabbi Brooks Susman. I am deeply indebted to the library staffs at Fordham, Columbia, Rutgers, Gettysburg Lutheran Seminary, and especially the interlibrary loan department at my home institution of Kean University, which also provided release time for the research that got this project started. At Paulist Press, I am grateful to Mark-David Janus, CSP, Donna Crilly, and the entire production and marketing team for accepting and shepherding this project to completion. I am especially thankful that Paul McMahon agreed to turn his deft editorial hand to the manuscript.

I'm especially grateful to the elders among this list, some of whom I have known since my childhood. One person, a laicized Catholic priest now in his seventies whom I served more than thirty years ago as an altar boy, ratified my decision to dare take up this book project when I was still in my forties. After reading through the manuscript, he wrote to me, "Just as young Elihu could address his elders, Job and his friends, and remind them of the gifts that are bestowed freely, so you, Christopher, have been able to tell me in this book: 'Be quiet, "Fr. Ed," the journey is still a pilgrimage, and you are not alone, and you are not silent, and you are still able to learn and give to others.'" I offer this book not from my own abilities, then, but by drawing on what many others have taught—and continue to teach—me.

At the start of a book on aging, I now turn to a young girl. My wife and I named our daughter well: on a particularly frustrating writing day when she was 4 years old, Grace handed me a short, thick, yellow crayon and said, "Here, Daddy, this will help you write your book." May she always share the generosity of her wise old soul, a blessing from her mother. And so finally, and as always, I thank Karen, my wife and my best friend, for being her and for helping me be me.

A Note on Biblical Texts

For most of my research, I used the New Revised Standard Version (NRSV) of the Bible. Because I wanted to draw on scriptural texts that provided further insight to our subject, I turned to the New American Bible (NAB) for the seven books and sections of others that Protestants and Jews do not count among their canon of Hebrew Scripture. These are known as Deuterocanonical books in Catholic circles and apocrypha to Protestants and Jews. For this study, relevant NAB texts include Wisdom, Sirach (also known as ben Sirach/ben Sira or Ecclesiasticus—not to be confused with Ecclesiastes), and two additional chapters at the end of Daniel.

Part I

Cultivating Wisdom

"This is wisdom: it is the grace of being able to see everything with the eyes of God."

—Pope Francis

Before we explore lessons on wisdom from the Bible, we must take a moment to lay out a road map. In this part, we begin by providing an overview. We must first deal with a fundamental biblical paradox that we will encounter repeatedly on our journey: Does wisdom come with age? What kind of attitude should we embrace when we hear biblical stories that just can't be true of people living hundreds of years? Are there insights to be gathered about wisdom and experience from other eras and cultures? Can we develop an open-minded wisdom from Socrates or others who never read the Bible?

Chapter 1

Biblical Paradoxes

As we walk on our spiritual journeys, who teaches us how to grow in wisdom? The Bible is one place where we can learn from wise characters who can teach us their insights. Often, we will find that experienced women and men have the most to teach—we might call them the wise elders of the Bible. However, we will also find young people speaking with wisdom, too, and often others will say, "They speak like wise old people." As we will see shortly, in fact, the Book of Job tells us that sometimes "it is not the old that are wise, / nor the aged that understand what is right" (Job 32:9).

The Bible is a shared cultural text for those of many faiths or even none at all. Believer or not, almost everyone knows the Sunday school stories. *Ageless Wisdom* explores familiar and overlooked stories and sayings from the Bible to share lessons for today's readers. What wisdom did biblical people learn from their experiences? What can they teach us today as we travel our own paths toward greater wisdom?

The takeaway:

- Bible heroes and heroines earned wisdom from their failures and flaws as much as from their successes and triumphs.

- The wisdom that comes from experience can be both a blessing and a grace-filled burden.
- There is a particular wisdom that comes from humility—a lost virtue.
- The biblical school of hard knocks cultivates the savvy wisdom of bargaining and of waiting.
- We must learn to laugh with the wise perspective of a life lived with our eyes wide open.
- When we see our heroes in their golden years, they not only reap the good they have sown, but they pay it forward: they sow the seeds of their wisdom for their children and grandchildren to harvest.

We should not be surprised to find reverence for the wise in an ancient culture such as that of the Bible. Ethnographers have long known that experience brings with it prestige in many cultures. Often in the ancient and medieval past, that prestige is related to knowledge, magic, and religious insight. Elders keep the past as storytellers. They transmit a culture's identity to the next generation—much as Homer told the tales of Troy centuries after the events. In plays and myths from ancient Athens to Shakespeare's nurse in *Romeo and Juliet*, wise sages bring messages from the gods, offer good advice (that the proud young usually ignore), and interpret oracles and dreams. We think of medieval and modern-day wizards from Merlin to Dumbledore and Gandalf, Asian sages like China's Confucius, and writers like America's Mark Twain and Maya Angelou. We turn to them not for instant analysis but for long-term experience and perspective born from traveling rocky roads.

In its own time and ours, the Bible asks us to revere these wise men and women, to learn from their lives and their stories, and to understand that, as a result of their years of experience and heartache, they are keepers of wisdom. Diodorus Siculus, a Greek historian, put it this way: "Knowledge of history...endows the young with the wisdom of the aged."[1] But Diodorus Siculus didn't quite get his biblical wisdom lessons right, which isn't entirely his fault, since he was writing about 60–30 BCE—just when the Old Testament was finishing up and the New Testament was about to begin.

The Bible is complex. While the wisdom of the aged is a large part of our story, it is not the only part. We will also meet folks who are young and wise. *Ageless Wisdom* plays with the relationship between age and wisdom as it aims to draw biblical lessons for today. Biblical wisdom, then, must also be about biblical aging—and, by extension, about what later people reading the Bible thought about wisdom and aging. To take aging out of a conversation about biblical wisdom would be like making a sandwich without the bread.

THE BIBLE IS A LIVING TEXT

The Bible is a living text—it's not fixed in time. Every generation and culture tries to own the Bible's stories by retelling and reinterpreting them for their own place and time. However, first it is essential to place biblical tales, myths, legends, allegories, and proverbs in the context of the ancient biblical world in which they were written as chronicles and instructive stories. We must also explore how Jews, Christians, and Muslims appropriated these Bible stories and sayings over the centuries. How did generations living *after* the biblical age receive and apply these stories in order to find cautionary tales and guides for their own lives? Drawing on the Bible itself and also on ancient, medieval, and modern Jewish commentaries (*midrashim*), Christian sources, and Islamic prophetic tales (*Qiṣaṣ al-anbiyā* or *Tales of the Prophets*), we will track how past generations of men and women have made the biblical lessons about growing in wisdom their own. *Ageless Wisdom* offers a roadmap to learn from the Bible in our own contexts.

Turning to the Bible need not be tied to belief in God. An atheist will benefit from the Bible's lessons as much as a believer. The Bible is a shared cultural text regardless of faith tradition and can even teach those who follow no faith at all.[2] The Bible's stories are the world's stories—even to the point of sharing core tales. Is the prehistoric story of Cain killing Abel much different from Romulus killing Remus and establishing the city of Rome in 753 BCE? The biblical story of Noah recounts the flood while the polytheistic *Epic of Gilgamesh* tells of Utnapishtim, the Mesopotamian Noah who, like him, packed his family and a pair of every animal into an ark when instructed to do so by Ea, the god of intelligence and wisdom, in order to spare him from a massive deluge. These stories are our stories. They have been read and used by those who shaped ancient, medieval, and modern societies around the globe. Bible stories have helped make us and our world who and what we are.

Moreover, it is not necessary to regard the biblical stories as historical fact, as was the case for many centuries, in order to learn biblical lessons. When ancient and medieval Jews, Christians, and Muslims read these stories, they took them to have been actual events that gave insight, meaning, perspective, and understanding to their own contemporary lives. Some people today read the Bible as a history book. But there can be a kind of accuracy and truth even if the actual historical facts can't be proven. For example, no medieval scholar can prove that St. Francis of Assisi, who died in the early thirteenth century, actually said, "Preach the gospel. Use words if you must." Yet, the fact remains that his own activities and reputation as an *alter Christus*—another Christ—bear truth to this legendary statement that we teach more by our actions than by our words. Similarly, we don't have to accept that a young George Washington admitted to his father that he chopped down a cherry tree in order to understand that Washington was a man of uncommon virtue, honesty, and integrity—which is the point of the story, after all.

BIBLICAL PARADOXES

Centuries of scholarship have applied history, archaeology, philology, linguistics, manuscript studies, and other academic skills and methods to the Bible. Consequently, we now have a better but still-evolving sense of when the Bible was written, who wrote it, and how to approach the various challenges of interpreting Scripture. Still, the Bible is used sometimes as a weapon. Many want the Bible to say what *they* want it to say. Many want it to support what they already believe instead of seeing it as a guide and teacher. And many interpret it in black-and-white terms so that everyone else can think what they think. Fundamentally, many want the Bible to prove that they are right and that the other person is wrong.

However, this is not how the Bible works—and it certainly doesn't present wisdom in black-and-white language. Whether you believe that God is the Bible's author directly or that God inspired particular people to write its words, the fact remains that there is no consistent view of growing in wisdom in the Bible. Its many books were written at different times, in different contexts and cultures, by different authors with their own languages and voices based on their ages and backgrounds, in different genres, and for different reasons. The Bible is, in the end, an *anthology* where the wisdom of experience is mostly treated here and there, sometimes in direct focus, other times at the edge of a story, per-haps in a short word or phrase, or maybe elsewhere in a more extended treatment.[3]

The complexities, the reversals, and even the contradictions of the biblical paradoxes about wisdom can guide us to deeper lessons. Our world yearns for the black-and-white answer because it's simpler and clearer. However, what if simpler is really *simplistic*? Do we really want to follow ideas that are simplistic and watered down—and therefore likely untrue—or are we brave enough to stand in the messy middle and embrace the rich shades of gray in our lives? This is surely harder, but also more rewarding.

The prophet Job asks: "Is wisdom with the aged, / and understanding in length of days?" (Job 12:12). That, as Hamlet would say, is the question. And the conclusive answer, at least in this book of the Bible, is not the one you'd expect. In an exchange that we will explore later, insight comes from the mouth of the *youngest* person talking with Job. Few of us would be familiar with the name Elihu. However, it is Elihu—the Unknown, we might say—who waits respectfully until his elders have spoken before blasting them with a hard truth: "It is not the old that are wise, / nor the aged that understand what is right" (Job 32:9). That's humbling.

The essential lesson of our walk through the Bible and later centuries is that wisdom does not always come with age. But that fact shouldn't disappoint us. It makes perfect sense. A fool at twenty can still be a fool at eighty years of age. On the one hand, a person can live a life of virtue and be revered as virtuous in old age; on the other hand, you can be full of vice in youth and a jerk your whole life, but don't expect to turn into a wise elder just because you reach sixty. You can also have wisdom in your youth but also be a foolish old king. Our later years need not be either a blessing or a burden, but in fact are often both at the same time. Boldness may come from physical infirmity. In the pages that follow, we will see Jacob be bluntly honest to his children; it might make us cringe, but he's telling the truth. Abraham and Moses have lived enough to know that they can bargain with God. When told at the age of ninety that she's pregnant, Sarah laughs. Wouldn't you?

In the Book of Ruth, it's typically Ruth who is the heroine, caring for her elderly mother-in-law, Naomi, with affection and devotion. But from our reading of the episode, it's the older, over-looked widow, Naomi—the character who is typically a side fig-ure, a passive object, a pitiful old lady—who emerges as the wise and savvy woman. Naomi knows a good opportunity when she sees it and jumps to take advantage of the situation. Older Naomi is calling the shots; young Ruth is just doing what she's told.

We will also meet Barzillai, whom even most Bible readers probably won't recall as a household name. Earlier in his life, he'd helped a young David (later the famous king). While visiting the king in his palace in Jerusalem many years later, Barzillai turns down David's offer of a cushy retirement in the capital. He's no longer dazzled by riches and luxury. Humble Barzillai, who appears only in passing, will offer one of the most poignant and appealing biblical examples of an older fellow who sees the world with eyes wide open. He is at peace with himself, his life, and the world.

For another example of wisdom, this time outside the Bible, we need only turn to the Greek philosopher Socrates, who died in 399 BCE. (In this book, we will sometimes look at a few examples from outside the Bible that illuminate its lessons, too.) Socrates seems to understand better than most people the essential tie between wisdom and humility. Our episode begins when Socrates hears that the god, Apollo, through the popular and influential oracle at Delphi, declared him to be the wisest person around. The philosopher's response is amazement:

> I said to myself, "What is the god saying, and what is his hidden meaning? I am only too conscious that I have no claim to wisdom, great or small; so what can he mean by asserting that I am the wisest man in the world? He cannot be telling a lie; that would not be right for him."

Socrates does what he does best: he walks around and asks questions. Socrates goes to one fellow in particular and engages this politician in one of his typically probing dialogues only to discover "that although in many people's opinion, and especially in his own, he appeared to be wise, in fact he was not." This is disturbing to those standing around listening. No doubt the politician himself is none too pleased to have been publicly proven a fraud. (*Wouldn't this be fun today?*) Socrates draws insight from the scene:

> I reflected as I walked away: "Well, I am certainly wiser than this man. It is only too likely that neither of us has any knowledge to boast of; but he thinks that he knows something which he does not know, whereas I am quite conscious of my ignorance. At any rate it seems that I am wiser than he is to this small extent, that I do not think that I know what I do not know."[4]

"Ignorance is the beginning of wisdom" is often the way this episode is shortened into a proverb, one which has been attributed to many sages in diverse cultures from Socrates in ancient Greece to early America's Benjamin Franklin and beyond. Surely Socrates and Franklin knew, too, that there is a difference between factual knowledge and insightful wisdom. Consider all the facts you can find on the Internet. If you knew all of them, you'd have a pile of information. That might make you smart. But even with the largest pile of information, without judgment and the ability to make sense of all of those facts, you wouldn't have understanding. You wouldn't be wise.

Think of the smartest person you know. Now think of the wisest person you know. They probably aren't the same person. Finally, ask yourself: if you had to make a life-changing decision, would you go to the smartest person you know or to the wisest?

The first step on the journey of wisdom is to find what you don't know and to begin from there with no illusions. In several places, the Bible repeats the notion to say that "fear of the Lord" — best understood as humble reverence or awe — is a good start. The psalmist states,

> The fear of the LORD is the beginning of wisdom;
>> all those who practice it have a good understanding.
>>> (Ps 111:10)

Proverbs 1:7 adds a contrast with foolishness and reminds us that we need to continue learning:

> The fear of the LORD is the beginning of knowledge;
>> fools despise wisdom and instruction.

Proverbs 9:11 ties reverence and wisdom with the gift of long life:

> For by me [Wisdom] your days will be multiplied,
>> and years will be added to your life.

So let's not be afraid to explore the messy mysteries inside paradoxes like the one that says the beginning of wisdom is ignorance. As we proceed, we will encounter paired biblical paradoxes like the ones just mentioned — blessings and burdens, wisdom and humility — before examining how some biblical characters capitalized on their experience to draw on its gifts: the boldness to bargain with God along with perspective, patience, and a sense of humor. Finally, we will discover the Bible's lesson that every moment of our life is not only a chance to reap, but also an opportunity to sow.

Chapter 2

Gathering Wisdom

DOES LIFE BEGIN AT 140?

The Bible presents some truly bizarre long lives. We must deal with these head-on in order to understand them as simply meaning metaphorically "a fullness of years." Impossibly long lives are "unhistorical and mythological," as one scholar put it.[1] Genesis 5 and 11, for example, reveal a litany of familiar and not-so-famous names and ages: "All the days that Adam lived were nine hundred thirty years; and he died"; "When Adam had lived one hundred thirty years, he became the father of a son in his likeness, according to his image, and named him Seth...all the days of Seth were nine hundred twelve years; and he died"; "When Jared had lived one hundred sixty-two years he became the father of Enoch," and so on (see Gen 5:3–8, 18). Lifespans extend from Enoch's 365 years to Jared's 962 years. Fatherhood comes at age sixty-five (not surprising anymore to modern ears) to Methusaleh's 187 years of age. We have Arpachshad dying at 438 years and his son, Shelah, dying at 433 years, although both were fathers way back in their thirties, a far more reasonable number today (see Gen 11:12–15).

Methusaleh is the Bible's oldest person, dying at 969, though curiously little else is mentioned about him. Methusaleh has attracted attention throughout the centuries. California's oldest trees are known as the Methusaleh grove. His very long life of almost a millennium caused the Italian humanist Petrarch to wonder if long life necessarily brought happiness—and concluded that this was not true. "If living long made us happy, the happiest of all would have been Methusaleh, which no one has ever said or believed," Petrarch wrote in 1363 to a friend named Neri Morando, the rumors of whose death had been greatly exaggerated (in Mark Twain style). "Not the quantity, but the quality of a life must be considered, nor do the length of years matter but the splendor of the deeds, and especially the end of life."[2]

Noah is an interesting character in himself, let alone the fact that his parents come in for some attention, too. His father, Lamech, fathers him at 182 years and dies at 777 years. His mother, named Cainush in a twelfth-century Islamic collection of stories, is asked her age by a potential suitor. She responds that she's 180 years. The suitor says that she's not mature enough, meaning that she wasn't menstruating yet according to the storyteller, who informs us that, in those days, puberty arrived at 200. If you were 200, the suitor says, I'd marry you, which makes Cainush come clean. "I thought you were not going to pay me any heed," she said, "but now that you want to marry me, I will tell you that I am actually two hundred and twenty years old." And so they marry and have Noah.[3] He fathers three boys named Ham, Shem, and Japheth at 500 years, making him the oldest father in the Bible. He builds the ark at 600 and dies at 950 years, not quite able to stretch out to his grandfather Methusaleh's record.

Other cultures in biblical times indicate long lives, too. Herodotus, a fifth-century BCE Greek historian who gullibly wrote down every good story he heard without checking it out first, includes in his *Histories* some ancient tall tales. Herodotus records that the Massagetae, a people who likely lived somewhere in central Asia, practiced a kind of glorious going away party with the guest of honor doubling as the main course. "When a man is very old, all his relatives give a party and include him in a general sacrifice of cattle; then they boil the flesh and eat it. This they consider to be the best sort of death. Those who die of disease are not eaten but buried, and it is held a misfortune not to have lived long enough to be sacrificed." Herodotus also informs us with a straight face that most Ethiopians lived to be at least 120 years. They traced their source of long life to an Ethiopian fountain of youth—a spring, Herodotus tells us, whose water "smelled like violets and caused a man's skin, when he washed in it, to glisten as if he had washed in oil. They said the water of this spring lacked density to such a degree that nothing would float in it, neither wood nor any lighter substance—everything sank to the bottom. If this account is true, then their constant use of it must be the cause of the Ethiopians' longevity." Cleitarchus, writing late in the fourth century BCE about Alexander the Great's journeys east, recounts stories of people in India living between 100 and 200 years old.[4]

Most remarkably, Sumerian kings had ages and reigns reaching tens of thousands of years, far outpacing Hebrew patriarchs and matriarchs. There is a King List dating to the reign of a fellow named Utu-hegal, about 2400 BCE. Like the Bible's story of Noah and the Flood, the King List indicates an event called the Deluge that's related in the *Epic of Gilgamesh*. That epic is a story transmitted, like Homer's *Iliad* and *Odyssey* about the Trojan War and its aftermath, by oral poets over centuries. They passed down legends about a king of Uruk named Gilgamesh reaching as far back, perhaps, as 2800 BCE. The King List says that, before the Deluge, kings lived and reigned over 25,000 years each. The longest was En-men-lu-Annak, who reigned for 43,200 years. Two others ruled for 36,000 years, two for 21,000 years, and still two more clocked in at 18,600 years—literally incredible but intriguing for a certain precision.

After the Deluge, the numbers drop, but individual Sumerian kings still reigned for hundreds and sometimes thousands of years, though never as long as before the Deluge. Parsing through the list, it is refreshing and interesting to find some reasonable numbers sprinkled in—reigns of eight, nine, fifteen, and thirty years with something of a standard of thirty-six years cropping up frequently. The numbers don't always diminish, however: short reigns are followed by others of 195, 360, 290, or 400 years. There is a woman named (as near as we can figure out) Ku(g)-Baba, a barmaid, though other translations have her referenced more entrepreneurially as a wine-woman, a female wine-seller, or hostess of a tavern. She apparently ruled as a monarch in Kish for a century, during which time she made her city stronger both economically and politically. And then there's a sort of queen mum: Adad-guppi', the mother of a mid-sixth–century BCE Babylonian ruler named Nabonidus, who was 102 or 104 at her death—once again, a precise number that teases our imagination for its possibility of accuracy.[5]

What are we to make of these large numbers, be they in the hundreds or even thousands of years of life? We shouldn't be surprised, after all, that in the urban theocracies of the world's first civilizations, we find temple prayers for a king's long life and good health, which in turn would guarantee peace and prosperity for the community. A sixth-century BCE Babylonian inscription ascribed to Nebuchadnezzar II relates a prayer to Marduk, the chief god: "May I attain old age within [the temple], and may I be fulfilled with extreme old age."[6]

However, if they existed, why did the longest lifespans disappear? Some scholars have tried to take the question on quite seriously. The stories of Noah's Flood and the Deluge from the *Epic of Gilgamesh* make for interesting turning points during biblical times. After the Mesopotamian Deluge, according to the King List, no ruler reigned or lived for more than 1,560 years—still quite long, but 43,200 years it's not. There is an ancient Chinese explanation dating far back to the edges of recorded history. A Taoist ruler called the Yellow Emperor, a legendary figure from ca. 2700–2600 BCE who was also something of a physician, wondered in a dialogue with a heavenly mentor why no one in his day lived as long as their ancestors had:

> I hear the ancient people did not decline in health even when they were over one hundred years old. However the present people become decrepit at just over fifty. Why is this?
>
> Because the present people do not pay attention to natural law [and instead] pursue pleasure and exhaust themselves before they accomplish their natural life span. On the contrary, the ancient people lived according to what they should be (the Perfect), that is natural law, so they could accomplish a celestial longevity.

A Benedictine abbot named Engelbert of Admont (ca. 1250–1331) offered a similar moral explanation as to why human beings had lived so long before the Flood. He speculated that it was due to a combination of God's will, pure air and water, and healthy plants. Lifespans shortened before the Flood because people were giving in to the very lusts and desires that motivated God to send forty days and nights of rain to purify the world. Engelbert believed that as time passed from the period when human beings lived in the Garden of Eden, human lifespans shortened because people were that much further removed from their original perfect state with God. In his time, the abbot labeled the first thirty-five years of life as that of youth, followed by fifteen years of status quo, then a long thirty-five years of old age ending in death at about eighty-five years.

In the sixteenth century, the German religious reformer Martin Luther also looked to Paradise and the Flood to explain how long people lived in the Bible as compared to his own time. For Luther it seemed that we'll never get back to the state of perfection and full knowledge of God that we enjoyed there. "Before Noah's flood, the world was highly learned, by reason men lived a long time, and so attained great experience and wisdom; now, ere we begin rightly to come to the true knowledge of a thing, we lie down and die." But, according to Luther, it appears that this fact is not due to human intellectual laziness or satisfaction, but to God's will: "God will not have that we should attain a higher knowledge of things."[7] Apparently, we'll never enjoy Eden again.

With the onset of the Scientific Revolution, some theorists looked for a more technical and less religious or moral interpretation of declining lifespans in the context of the age of the universe and planet. Robert Hooke, a seventeenth-century English natural philosopher, posited that friction made the speed of Earth's rotation slow down over the centuries, leading to modern years being longer than those in prehistoric and biblical eras. In earlier centuries, in other words, years were shorter. Thomas Burnet, a seventeenth-century chaplain to Great Britain's King William III, offered a geological explanation, but one still grounded in a belief that Noah's story is true: the Flood shifted the Earth's axis. Before this happened, it was spring all the time, so it was easier to live longer; after the Earth's axis was shifted by the Flood, other seasons came into being and made life harder. Other early modern theories speculated that patriarchs lived a long time because the newly formed Earth needed to be filled with people. Once population levels filled the land and stabilized, lifespans shortened on their own account so the world would not have a surplus population that it couldn't sustain.[8]

A LIFETIME ROAD TO WISDOM

We want to believe that in those long ago, mythic, good-old biblical days, elders were revered for the wisdom they learned and earned. Maybe thinking that way makes us feel better since our own era bursts with an urgent sense of the importance of "now" and instantaneous communication. We throw away what doesn't work anymore. We don't even expect our technology to last more than a few years—we'll just buy the new version when it comes out. The luster of an ancient culture of respect is alluring, if only to make ourselves feel virtuous. We imagine elders teaching their communities in prehistoric and biblical times as well as traditional family settings ranging from African tribes to extended families in Asia and the Americas.

However, biblical people did not always honor the aged as keepers of wisdom. Yahweh lays down the fifth well-known rule in the Ten Commandments, "Honor your father and mother"—a commandment, however, that continues with an ancient incentive that's not often mentioned. We should honor our parents "so that your days may be long in the land that the LORD your God is giving you" (Exod 20:12). The young should honor the elderly, if only because—as that less-familiar second part of the fifth commandment puts it—the young's reward will be long life. To jump ahead in place and time, a Native American Ojibway proverb agrees: "Honor the aged; in honoring them, *you* have life and wisdom." The Qur'an likewise commands, "Thy Lord hath decreed…that ye be kind to parents. Whether one or both of them attain old age in thy life, say not to them a word of contempt, nor repel them, but address them in terms of honour." And lest a Muslim son or daughter fail to comply, the Qur'an reminds them of a child's debt to a parent: "And, out of kindness, lower to them the wing of humility, and say: "'My Lord! bestow on them thy Mercy even as they cherished me in childhood'" (*Sura* 17:23–24).⁹

Polytheistic Greeks and Romans also had to be goaded into caring for the elderly. Adult children had to be legally bound to care for their parents; candidates for public office were checked to see that they had, indeed, fulfilled their obligations toward their parents. One of the laws of Solon, the great lawgiver of Athens who flourished in the sixth-century BCE, stipulated that if an Athenian did not care for his parents, he would lose his rights as a citizen—a fate worse than death for an Athenian. In the Hebrew and Greco-Roman cultures, the old were honored because of their past accomplishments—what they'd already done as young people—and not for any wisdom or achievement attached to the fact of their being old.¹⁰

So what, then, was the ideal age if it wasn't old age? In Mesopotamia, a set of writings called the *Sultantepe Tablets*, dating perhaps from the early first millennium BCE, records forty as the prime of life, death at fifty as a short life, sixty as a mature or excellent age, seventy as long life, eighty as old age, and ninety as a time of might (a curious and unexplained ending). The Mishnah is a collection of rabbinic commentaries on Jewish teachings and law dating from about 200 CE. A section known as *Pirke Avot* or *Ethics of the Fathers* (or *Sages*) labels seventy as the time for gray hair, eighty as an age of special strength, ninety as the time of a bowed back, and one hundred being as good as dead. An interesting parallel to this last figure comes from Christian Scripture: In Romans 4:19, Paul seems to illustrate how first-century CE folks saw lifespans back in the time of Genesis. The passage states that Abraham "was already as good as dead (for he was about a hundred years old)" when God told him and Sarah that they would have a child (Gen 17:5).¹¹

Many ancient thinkers believed that the world as well as the individual human being passed through successive stages of life—often numbered as three or seven—or that they were tied together in seasons in a kind of macrocosm-microcosm linkage. For the Greeks, following the views of Pythagoras in the sixth century BCE, childhood was spring, a lad enjoyed summer, a young man lived in fall, and an old man died in winter. Solon proposed a system of ten weeks of years culminating—yet again—in that particular age of seventy. He believed that we're strongest in insight and speech from ages forty-nine to sixty-three; while a person was not done at sixty-three, the next seven years represented winding down to a timely death at seventy. In a depressing passage in his *Rhetoric*, Aristotle, a few centuries later, declared forty-nine to be the intellectual peak of a human life, noting that, as we move further from that number, elderly people become more unsure, cynical, distrustful, suspicious, petty, cheap, cowardly, fearful, proud, impotent, and quick to be angry but also prone to feeble and pitiful attempts at rage. In an interesting parallel from the east, a death before sixty in Indian culture is called untimely: a bad death is the result of a bad life full of sin and bad karma. A longer life allows more time for enlightenment: the older a person becomes, the greater potential for more enlightenment and wisdom. At the same time, echoing Aristotle, we find that the Hindi word *sathiyana*, which can be translated as "sixty-ish" or "to go sixty-ish," implies forgetfulness.

Christians did not throw away Greco-Roman notions linking the life of the world with human ages, but baptized them with their own interpretation. The North African bishop and theologian, Augustine of Hippo (354–430), positioned the sixth age in his world scheme with the moment when Jesus would return in the Second Coming. Augustine calibrated this universal era to old age in a human life. Echoing Paul in 2 Corinthians 4:16 ("Even though our outer nature is wasting away, our inner nature is being renewed day by day."), Augustine taught that old age wastes away the outer body at the same time that the inner person is renewed every day of his or her life. Augustine believed old age arrived at sixty, but could last another sixty years—as long as the prior stages of life combined—ending with death as late as 120 years old. A Spanish bishop named Isidore of Seville (ca. 560–636) was also a bit more optimistic. He said that life gets good at fifty years; the next two decades are full of maturity until old age starts at seventy years.

Jewish sources, like Greco-Roman pagan and Christian ideas, also linked human ages to nature. A Jewish anthology known as *Ecclesiastes Rabbah* has a colorful seven-part framework that tied ages to animals. At three we roll in the mud like a pig, at ten we jump around like young goats, in marriage we are lazy like an ass, in parenthood we protect our children like a mother animal tends her litter, and in old age we're wrinkled like apes.[12]

In Elizabethan England, Shakespeare's *Sonnet 2* makes it sound like it's all over at forty: we're already old and done with wrinkles like crow's feet. But at least the Bard stresses that our children can carry on our beauty and be our heritage. See your children, Shakespeare consoles us, and you see your bloodline continuing on:

> This were to be new-made when thou art old,
> And see thy blood warm when thou fell'st it cold.

Likely drawing on this long tradition of linking ages with periods of life and the world, Shakespeare also adopted the seven ages of man model in *As You Like It*. In his "all the world's a stage" speech (Act II, scene 7), the character Jaques looks to old age and the end of life, even if he does so with a depressing description reminiscent of Aristotle.

> Last scene of all,
> That ends this strange eventful history,

Is second childishness and mere oblivion;
Sans teeth, sans eyes, sans taste, sans everything.

The age of seventy years has a long history. In the Bible, seventy emerges as a model age—though not the only one. For example, Psalm 90:10 informs us that seventy is the ideal age of death—the proverbial three score and ten—but the psalmist also says that extraordinary strength can extend life to eighty: "The days of our life are seventy years, or perhaps eighty, if we are strong." Rashi (an acronym drawn from Rabbi Shlomo Yitzhaki), the eleventh-century French rabbi, looked at a prayer earlier in the collection of psalms, in this case Psalm 61:6, "Prolong the life of the king; may his years endure to all generations!" Rashi commented precisely that, "If it had been decreed for me to die as a youth, add days to my days so that my years will be 70 years." In eastern philosophy, too, seventy is an important age. Confucius (ca. 551–479 BCE), in his *Analects*, says of himself that it wasn't until he was seventy that he found balance between what was right for him and what was good for the community: "At 70, I could follow the dictates of my own heart; for what I desired no longer overstepped the boundaries of right."[13] Now that sounds like pretty sage advice worthy of following.

While we've seen 70, 80, or even 100 as prime ages to indicate a full and revered life, the metaphoric number 120 comes up, too. In Genesis 6:3, right after we read the genealogy from Adam to Noah, who allegedly lived for hundreds of years, we discover that God decided to put 120 years as the limit of a human life, especially for the people most worthy of blessing, honor, and reward. A particular Jewish blessing declares, "May you live to be 120." But we should notice that God decided not to hold to this limit of 120 years all the time. Abraham died at 175, Sarah at 127, three figures at 137 (Ishmael, Levi, and Amram—the last was Moses' father, apparently passing along good genes to his son),

Isaac at 180, Jacob at 147, Aaron at 123, Kohath at 133, and a high priest named Jehoiada at 130 with Joseph and Joshua curiously not quite making it to 120 since they both died at 110.

There is a Tannaitic tradition (referring to classic rabbinic commentaries of the third century CE) that Moses and three later Jewish sages died at 120. The three other sages were Hillel the Elder, Rabban Johanan ben Zakkai, and Rabbi Akiba, who lived at various periods from the first century BCE through the second century CE. This was a very transformative time in Jewish history. It was the period when Jesus lived and then the Romans destroyed Jerusalem before rebuilding it as a pagan center. Each of the four men spent the 120 years of their lives precisely in three parallel episodes of forty years each. Moses, for example, lived in Egypt and Midian for forty years each, and then was Israel's head for another forty years. As for the others: Hillel the Elder was forty years old when he came up to Jerusalem from Babylonia, served the Sages forty years, and led Israel for forty years; Rabban Johanan ben Zakkai was a merchant for forty years, served the Sages forty years, and led Israel for forty years; and Rabbi Akkiba was forty years old when he began to study Torah, served the Sages forty years, and led Israel forty years.

In another version of this commentary tradition, which enjoyed quite a prominent status through the Middle Ages, six pairs of sages (some familiar but most unknown) lived for 120 years. At the place where Moses' death, at precisely the 120-year-old maximum limit, is recorded in Deuteronomy 34:7, this commentary of collected rabbinical wisdom names the six pairs: Rebekah and Kohath, Levi and Amram, Joseph and Joshua, Samuel and Solomon, Moses and Hillel the Elder, Rabban Johanan ben Zakkai and Rabbi Akiba.[14]

LIVING ANCESTORS: A COMMUNITY'S WISDOM KEEPERS

Our cultural radar drives us to believe that wisdom keepers were always honored in ancient civilizations and that we should keep that reverence in our world today, too. We have already seen, however, that we have a mixed legacy to contend with if we are to be honest and not simplistic on our journey. We like to point out positive examples, of course. Among the Akan tribe in Ghana, for instance, age is indeed a mark of wisdom. Caring for the aged is the duty of everyone, not just the elders' children or grandchildren. It takes a village not only to raise a child, apparently, but also to honor the aged. For the Akan, the aged are considered "living ancestors" and "custodians of the moral, ethical, social, and legal life" of the community. As an Akan proverb puts it, "If someone nurses you to produce your teeth, you also nurse them when they begin to lose theirs." Age, for the Akan, is a sign of a good, honest, and genuine life.[15]

In China, both in the past and today, long life and wisdom are also revered, almost always at the same time. Filial piety in the Confucian system is everything. All must honor this duty; obedience and reverence are expected not only toward living people, but altars of ancestors, too—an interesting parallel with a statement by the Greek philosopher Plato, who in his *Laws* decrees that even a statue of an elder should be respected. In the *Classic of Filial Piety* (called the *Xiao Jing*), filial piety is absolutely foundational. It is one of the first things Chinese children learn at home and in school.

In serving his parents a filial son renders the utmost reverence to them while at home. In supporting them he maximizes their pleasure. When they are sick he takes every care. At their death he expresses all his grief. Then he sacrifices to them with full solemnity. If he has fulfilled these five requirements, then he is truly able to serve his parents.

Right relationships lead to order as between a father and son or between rulers and their people. To respect one's parents—and to do so willingly and with an attitude of respect, even to the detriment of your own obligations to yourself—is to contribute to order and to head off chaos so all may be well under Heaven.

We find a contemporary parallel in Buddhism. In *Sangala Sutta*, Buddha's discourse on family relationships, the young are directed to respect all elders because senior citizens are Brahma (the creator God). Sons and daughters are particularly charged with caring for their parents as they age, with maintaining their family's honor and wealth, and with fulfilling funeral duties. Caring and respecting is good for the older people, clearly, but it's also recognized as an honorable deed for those doing the caring and respecting, as it can lead to the reward of rebirth in good karma.[16]

However, as we have seen, when we look more closely at the understanding of aging through the ages, we also discover paradoxes like those in the Bible. In the past and today, we like to think that we honor living ancestors as wisdom keepers, but the truth often reveals a wider and deeper ambivalence. In ancient Greece, old age was honored in theory until the elderly became a burden in practice. Plato stipulated that elders should be held with respect, even awe, but that a man over forty who picks a fight or defends himself should be punished and demeaned—an image of feebleness surely comes to mind.[17]

Similarly, the wisdom and merits of experience were sometimes appreciated and revered. In ancient Sparta, for example, one of the most powerful governing bodies was the *Gerousia*, a word related to the Greek *geron*, meaning an old man; we get the name for the fields of geriatrics and gerontology from this root. The *Gerousia* was a council of elders comprised of the two sitting kings and twenty-eight elected men over the age of sixty who served for life. This powerful council controlled Sparta's legislative agenda, selecting which bills would go to the larger Assembly for votes; even then, its members retained a veto power over the Assembly's actions. The *Gerousia* also constituted the criminal court for the worst crimes like treason and homicide where the penalty was the loss of citizenship, exile, or death. Within the Assembly itself, those over fifty years were permitted to speak first, certainly a platform for their running for a spot in the *Gerousia* when they turned sixty.

Spartan respect stands out among the customary indifference, even disdain, for the elderly that we find among the rest of the Greeks. Male gods are sometimes old and bearded to demonstrate their power or wisdom, but their bodies represent a modern Mr. Olympia more than a real-life old man who might tend sheep on the slopes of Mt. Olympus. Geras, the ancient Greeks' male god representing old age, is depicted as a hobbled, thin, defenseless, vulnerable, and wrinkled fellow more to be pitied than worshipped or feared. There are hardly any depictions of older goddesses at all. One especially stands out by its negativity. In Hesiod's *Theogony*, we read about the birth of the gods. There, Night is named as the mother of Old Age, who is described as sad and accursed.[18]

One representative illustration of lip service paid to experience comes from Homer's *Iliad*, which dates from about the eighth century BCE. Older veterans in the stories of the Trojan War usually can't compete well in battle, but they have experience and some wisdom, as in the case of Nestor, whose years of combat and ruling bring him a measure of honor. In a key scene, Achilles and Agamemnon are bickering over a war bride named Briseis. Nestor, long revered as a persuasive speaker and wise counselor, stands between them. We know that he is old because Homer describes Nestor as having seen two generations after him die. Now he sees a third generation, who are his great-grandsons, at war. The aged warrior tries to keep peace among the Greeks so they can stand united against the Trojans.

In this scene, Nestor attempts to reason directly with Achilles and Agamemnon:

> Stop. Please.
> Listen to Nestor. You are both younger than I,
> and in my time I struck up with better men than you,
> even you, but never once did they make light of me…
> but they,
> they took to heart my counsels, marked my words.
> So now you listen too….

But when he is done talking so eloquently, nothing has changed. Achilles and Agamemnon have only paused to let Nestor speak: they take no mind of his words, picking up right where their shouting match had left off a moment before and storming off, divided just as Nestor had feared—and warned.[19]

They had missed Nestor's wisdom. Let's not make the same mistake.

Part II

Lessons and Gifts

"It's good for the elderly to communicate their wisdom to the young; and it is good for the young people to gather this wealth of experience and wisdom and to carry it forward."

—Pope Francis

As we begin our exploration of the Bible's lessons and gifts about wisdom, we will continue to encounter paradoxes. We might ask: If you are wise, why be humble about it? Once biblical characters began to appreciate what they had learned, they found themselves duty bound to share their lessons and gifts. They understood their bargaining power—even with God. They saw that blessings and grace could be pulled from their burdens. They learned the wisdom of patience and laughter. And their experiences allowed them not only to reap lessons for themselves, but to sow understanding and wisdom to others.

Chapter 3

Being Wise, Being Humble

THE LESSON OF ELIHU

We may have heard and be familiar with the story of Job, but here we will pay particular attention to a character in the story named Elihu, whom you may never have noticed. To review the story's main elements: Job is a loyal son of Yahweh and does everything right. For some unexplained reason, however, God decides to test Job. He loses his health, his family, everything that's precious to him—yet Job remains faithful to Yahweh. Because Job does not lose faith and instead accepts his incomprehensible, innocent suffering, Yahweh restores all that Job had lost and even doubles it, then grants him a long life. Job had ten children before his fortunes turned, then lived another 140 years after he was rewarded.

Much of the Book of Job follows a debate among Job and three of his friends with quite unusual names and hometowns: Eliphaz the Temanite, Bildad the Shuhite, and Zophar the

Namathite. They tell Job that he's wrong *not* to blame Yahweh. Job should instead be very angry.

On the other hand, a fourth, often overlooked friend, Elihu, takes a different approach. He starts by asking a key question for our own journey about biblical wisdom. Elihu poses the question this way:

> Is wisdom with the aged,
>> and understanding in length of days?
>
> (Job 12:12)

Elihu's answer is, "No":

> It is not the old that are wise,
>> nor the aged that understand what is right.
>
> (Job 32:9)

Elihu says that wisdom is with God. He stands with a number of psalms and proverbs that indicate wisdom begins by fearing the Lord and following divine rules, regardless of a person's age.

Job's other friends come from a different, more standard position. They say what we expect (and maybe want) them to say. Eliphaz the Temanite, speaking to Job, implies that age helps wisdom:

> Have you listened in the council of God?
>> And do you limit wisdom to yourself?
> What do you know that we do not know?
>> What do you understand that is not clear to us?
> The gray-haired and the aged are on our side,
>> those older than your father.
>
> (Job 15:8–10)

In his long rebuttal (Job 32—37), Elihu gets angry with the three friends Eliphaz, Bildad, and Zophar, along with Job. It's very important to notice that Elihu is aware of his own youth. He's anxious to join the debate, but as the youngest person present, he respectfully holds his tongue: "Now Elihu had waited to speak to Job, because they were older than he," but when his turn comes, Elihu holds nothing back:

> I am young in years,
>   and you are aged;
> therefore I was timid and afraid
>   to declare my opinion to you.
> I said, "Let days speak,
>   and many years teach wisdom."
> But truly it is the spirit in a mortal,
>   the breath of the Almighty, that makes for
>   understanding.
> It is not the old that are wise,
>   nor the aged that understand what is right.
>   (Job 32:4–9)

And then Elihu, though younger, tells Job to shut up and listen:

> Pay heed, Job, listen to me;
>   be silent, and I will speak.
> If you have anything to say, answer me;
>   speak, for I desire to justify you.
> If not, listen to me;
>   be silent, and I will teach you wisdom.
>   (Job 33:31–33)

After Elihu rebukes Job and the three friends, he offers praise for God's goodness, greatness, and justice while criticizing self-righteous people. His core message is that living according to God's plan is what brings health, joy, long life—and wisdom.

If they listen, and serve him,
>they complete their days in prosperity,
>and their years in pleasantness.
But if they do not listen, they shall perish by the sword,
>and die without knowledge.

>(Job 36:11–12)

Elihu understood the disconnect between a regular reckoning of time by the calendar and what's been called God's time. The ancient Greeks did, too. They had two contrasting conceptions of time: *chronos* and *kairos*. *Chronos* is chronological time—the hours and minutes on your watch or cellphone, the way we measure our time on earth by days and dates on a calendar. *Kairos* is time-out-of-time—unanticipated moments of insight where we feel snatched away from time and place. It might be the moment we fall in love, when our children are born, or an instance when we receive an unexpected and unearned kindness. It's that booster shot of grace out of nowhere. We grind out our daily lives according to *chronos*, but our learning, insights, and revelations—our *Aha!* moments—are marked by a spark of *kairos*. *Chronos* advances our age. *Kairos* imparts wisdom.

MORE PARADOXES

We've just heard a biblical story that turns one of our most fundamental assumptions about age and wisdom on its head. Let's be kind to ourselves though. Our assumption isn't unwarranted because the Bible does speak of this connection. Psalm 90:12 instructs, "So teach us to count our days / that we may gain a wise heart." In the Book of Proverbs, we read,

Happy are those who find wisdom,
and those who get understanding,
For her income is better than silver,
and her revenue better than gold.
She is more precious than jewels,
and nothing you desire can compare with her.
Long life is in her right hand;
in her left hand are riches and honor.
Her ways are ways of pleasantness,
and all her paths are peace.
She is a tree of life to those who lay hold of her;
those who hold her fast are called happy.
(Prov 3:13–18)

And again, a few chapters later, we hear:

For by me [wisdom] your days will be multiplied,
and years will be added to your life.
(Prov 9:11)

In some cultures, as we have seen, elders are indeed revered as sages and dispensers of sound, wise judgement based on long experience—or at least that's what we want to think, so we focus on those examples that confirm our preconceived opinions. But as in many other sources, ancient to modern, we find an essential ambivalence: the sense of the elderly as wise, serene, and worthy of being counselors, but just as often being treated as mentally or physically frail and as a burden to younger people. Even in Jewish sources, with its biblical heritage of honoring the elderly—"You shall rise before the aged, and defer to the old" (Lev 19:32)—old age is generally described in negative terms, though specific older people are treated with respect. Men are mentioned as bent over, walking with a cane, and forgetful. At the same time, some medieval rabbis taught that in most social settings, the older person—simply by virtue of having passed more years than others—should be recognized with signs of honor. Others should stand when an older gentleman enters a room, for instance, and he should be allowed to sit at the head of a table when eating and to speak first in a meeting where decisions are to be made.

Nevertheless, the stereotype of the doddering old person has persisted from antiquity through the Middle Ages and into our own allegedly enlightened world. For some secular examples, we turn to Chaucer's writings from the late 1300s, where we find several typical stories of the cuckolded old man with a young, sultry wife. These are stock characters in the medieval genre called *fabliaux*, which were slapstick comic tales for the hooting crowd. A closer look at *fabliaux*, especially several of Chaucer's *Canterbury Tales*, reveals them to be examples of cruel humor at the expense of the elderly. In his *Merchant's Tale*, a prime and not-so-subtle example, an old man named January marries May, a young woman who has sex with another man right in front of her old husband. In the *Miller's Tale*, another old husband, in this case a carpenter named John, marries the eighteen-year-old Alison and takes in a boarder named Nicholas. Alison and Nicholas conspire to have sex while John, fooled by a rumor of a flood, sets up a kind of lifeboat as an escape. While Alison and Nicholas enjoy themselves, John falls and breaks his arm to the delight of his mocking neighbors. In the *Reeve's Tale*, although the father is not identified as particularly old, a familiar story is told: a miller cheats two young men, who fool him and have sex with his daughter in the miller's own bedroom.

Not every Chaucer story is so depressing for old folks: let's look at two more of his tales. First, in a morality *exemplum* titled the *Pardoner's Tale*, an old man wants either to exchange his many years for youth or to die. Though he's traveled as far as India, he can find no takers nor will death end his life. So he grows ever older until the day three young drunks harass him, which makes him chide them by using the biblical warning, "You shall rise before the aged" (Lev 19:32). The old man, no fool, recognizes greed, foolishness, and inexperience in their youth. When they say they want to find Death, who has taken away their friend, the old man tells the three just where to go: a certain tree nearby where eight bushels of gold sit underneath. No sooner do they find the gold that they plot against each other and all three end up dying in turn. In a sense, the wily old man triumphs: he outwits the young, who earn death earlier than they should. We hear no more of this elderly fellow, but it's possible to enjoy the idea that, in the end, it is he who has won the day, if not their youth or his own death.

A second interesting character and tale for our exploration is the wife of Bath. She fooled her first three husbands, who were old and rich—and therefore, she says, "good." Her latest husband is twenty years old to her forty, not quite old but, in medieval terms, moving along in years, and she discovers that she's no longer the boss in her marriage. Worse still, this young man is poor and has taken possession of her money, leading to physical brawls, which might be a bit of gender turnaround-is-fair-play in Chaucer's eyes. In the wife of Bath's tale, a knight meets a hag, who says he can have her young and beautiful (and take his chances that she'll be true to him, which we've seen is not likely in *fabliaux*) or old and faithful. The knight—indecisive or shrewd depending on your interpretation—lets her decide, at which point she becomes not only young but faithful in a conclusion celebrating the best of both worlds.

So, according to Chaucer, who stands for so much of popular literature and the thinking of the common person, old people of any historical period stand as a warning to young men and women who are lusty and full not only of life but also deception. These young fools delude themselves with the notion that there are no consequences to their actions. In Chaucer's tales, along with other similar stories from the Middle Ages, old age is typically punishment or penance. The elderly fear being taken advantage of, even attacked, by callous kids. Death as a release from suffering and pain even as people fear death's arrival is quite a common experience in the human condition dating back to some of the earliest writings dealing with aging and dying. But that's not to say that every now and again, as in the tales told by the pardoner and the wife of Bath, the old person's wise insight doesn't come through.[1] But we must listen to hear the wisdom.

Let's return to a biblical example that makes the point. The large and prestigious kingdom that David and Solomon had built ended up collapsing. We learn that Rehoboam, who was David's grandson and Solomon's son, lost his throne when he foolishly chose to ignore the wise advice given by the court's experienced advisers (1 Kgs 12:1–19; 2 Chr 10:1–19). They had served the wise king Solomon for a very long time and knew what paths were sure and which would lead to defeat. These older men advise Rehoboam to deal gently with his people. The king should act like their servant, listening to their words and lightening their load. On the other hand, the young men surrounding King Rehoboam go into macho mode. These are his friends since boyhood, now clearly enjoying their newfound power and influence since it is Rehoboam's turn on Israel's throne. These young and inexperienced counselors advise Rehoboam to crudely tell his people, "My little finger is thicker than my father's loins."

Rehoboam listens to the young advisers and does exactly the opposite of what the old men counsel. He makes his people's loads heavier, telling the nation of Israel, "My father disciplined you with whips, but I will discipline you with scorpions." Not surprisingly, a rebellion rises up. When Rehoboam sends Adoram, an overseer, to talk to the people, they stone the royal representative to death. Rehoboam stops strutting and starts running. Once again, this little-known biblical episode tells us much about wisdom. Even if you are a new king full of life, vigor, and a legitimate claim to an important throne, if you ignore the advice of seasoned counselors who know what they're talking about, you just might lose everything.

DON'T WASH THE GRAY OUT

Are there any clues that a person is wise? One indication of the wisdom that's supposed to accompany long life is white or gray hair, as illustrated in this essential biblical passage:

> How becoming to the gray-haired is judgment,
>   and a knowledge of counsel to those on in years!
> How becoming to the aged is wisdom,
>   understanding and prudence to the venerable!
> The crown of old men is wide experience;
>   their glory, the fear of the Lord.
>
> (Sir 25:4–6)

Proverbs, yet again, supports the notion that old age and wisdom are yoked together, in this case, illustrated by gray hair.

> Gray hair is a crown of glory;
>   it is gained in a righteous life.
>
> (Prov 16:31)

And once more:

> The glory of youths is their strength,
>   but the beauty of the aged is their gray hair.
>
> (Prov 20:29)

In the Ancient Near East of Mesopotamia, the general time and place where large chunks of the Bible were written, white or gray hair was considered so prestigious a mark of age and wisdom that some younger folks dyed their hair these colors—reversing our own tendency to rinse the gray out. In Sumeria, a woman with gray hair rose in honor and was sought out as a counselor. As a sage, diviner, priestess, or interpreter of dreams, she gave advice that was ignored at the listener's peril. In the Hebrew system, assigning numerical values to letters called *gematria*, the phrase "ripe old age" (*bakelah*), used often in the Bible and later Jewish literature, comes to the number 60, which links with just about the right age for wisdom and honor as far as demographic statistics of the time indicate.[2]

Where did the correlation between wisdom and old age as symbolized by gray hair first come from? The answer, it appears, is Abraham, according to a story found in a scriptural commentary genre called *midrash aggadah*, which is a later Jewish interpretation of a biblical episode. Abraham, so the story goes, was not getting the respect he deserved: "Until Abraham's time the young and old were not distinguishable from each other; consequently, young people would jest with Abraham, taking him for their companion." This situation annoyed Abraham, which we can certainly understand, and he prayed "for an outward token of dignity and honor for those advanced in years." Yahweh listened: "The Lord, granting his wish, said, 'You shall be the first upon whose head the silver crown of old age shall rest.'"[3]

Once again we come to a biblical paradox. In every age and community, there have been and always will be young people who are wiser than their years. We have the expression "she was born forty." Yet even when we have a person wise beyond her years, we often get a visual cue that the young person is recognized as worthy of giving counsel precisely because of a certain demeanor or gray hair. For example, though he's a young boy, the prophet Daniel commands respect because he reminds others of a wise old man. "Come, sit with us and inform us," the elders tell Daniel, "for God has given you the standing of an elder" (Dan 13:50). Another story is even more explicit about the visual cue. It seems that an eighteen-year-old named Eleazer ben Azariah was elected president of the Sanhedrin, the influential Jewish council. Challenged as too young for such an important position by some, his beard turned white and he declared, "Lo. I am like to one who is seventy years old."[4]

In the Christian tradition, we have several examples of old-young men distinguished by their white hair, literally or figuratively. We're told that, in the late fourth and early fifth century CE in the area that's now France, an archbishop named Honoratus, and his brother, Venantius, tried to move to another region, but their followers stood in the way: "For all their homeland felt that it was losing fathers in these youths. And indeed, they had attained to an old age that was not white-haired, but white with graces, and seen, not in withered limbs, but in lovely dispositions." Elsewhere, we hear that people said of these young brothers, "And what serious minds they had already acquired! And, with them, the mature wisdom of old men." About the same time, in Milan, a learned bishop named Ambrose took up the apparent contradiction: "Thus even in childhood there is a sort of venerable old age of behavior, and in old age a childlike innocence, because there is a form of old age which is venerable not by its duration, and which is not calculated by the number of years." Pope Gregory the Great wrote a biography of St. Benedict, the influential sixth-century monk, and described him as being old even when he was young. "From his younger days," Gregory says, Benedict "carried always the mind of an old man."[5]

Consequently, we have several stories about young men being wise that might seem to contradict the belief that wisdom comes with age. These young men carry authority before their time. And yet even here, we find a linkage between wisdom and age. Why else would we read about the gray or white hair growing literally or figuratively on their young heads? Why else would the young be praised for having the wisdom of the aged?

What Makes an Elder an Elder?

We expect that the very word *elder* denotes an older person of sound mind and solid judgement, with insights gained from experience. We're surprised to learn, however, that in many societies during and after biblical times, old age did not always qualify you as an elder, just as young age did not disqualify you. It's an interesting idea to pursue, since nearly every Ancient Near Eastern society included elders as a standard part of their social organization.[6]

One explicit example of the use of the word *elders* to describe chosen, trusted advisors occurs in the scene where Moses told Yahweh that his workload had become too much to carry alone. God responded favorably, directing Moses:

> Gather for me seventy of the elders of Israel, whom you know to be the elders of the people and officers over them; bring them to the tent of meeting, and have them take their place there with you. I will come down and talk with you there; and I will take some of the spirit that is on you and put it on them; and they shall bear the burden of the people along with you so that you will not bear it all by yourself. (Num 11:16–17)

Moses and God were simply doing what everyone else in that time and place did: choosing a community's natural and obvious leaders, seeking from them advice, direction, judgement, and decisions. These elders surely came from each community's informal, de facto network of the most important families in a particular region. Apparently, this was a standard process that worked in both Hebrew and polytheistic pagan communities like those of Mesopotamian societies. Recognizing elders based on wisdom and not age seems to have been the norm as time passed, cities emerged, and populations that required oversight and mediation grew. Elders served the functions of advisers, judges, arbitrators, negotiators, and ritual leaders. They surrounded and supported a leader, whatever his title may have been, and probably were sent by him to deal with other communities' leaders and elders as ancient ambassadors.

We find elders in Hebrew communities located far from the Temple in Jerusalem: the central site of liturgy and ritual, before and after Nebuchadnezzar destroyed Solomon's Temple in 587 BCE. Local leaders formed councils of elders to regulate Jewish life and to apply Jewish law to the different circumstances and locations where Hebrew communities were living away from their crushed capital. This pattern was followed quite logically with the earliest Christian communities that were made up mostly of Jews in the initial decades after Jesus' ministry. Jewish Christians simply carried their structures from one community to another. By the end of the first century CE, as Christian communities became overwhelmingly Gentile, it made sense to keep a structure of elders that worked quite nicely. Consequently, the earliest Christian communities had their own elders, who were referred to by various titles—later translated as *deacon, priest,* and *bishop*—though these titles did not have the same precise meaning as today.

But these elders were not always older. It is true that the root word in Hebrew for old age and aging (*zaken* or *zāqēn*) is closely aligned with the word for beard or elder, as in a man with a gray or white beard who is worthy of being called an elder. Employing this word carries the positive, conventional connotation that wisdom comes with age. More commonly, however, we learn that being an elder was more a measure of a man's judgement and standing, and not automatically of his age. The *body of elders* was typically taken as a plural word, as a group of people holding collective wisdom, and advanced age was not always considered as a factor. For the Hebrews of biblical times as well as for pagans of the same period, and Christians who followed, there was no necessary correlation between age and having the wisdom to be recognized and commissioned as a community elder. There could be a connection or relationship between the two, of course, but older age did not seem to be a mandatory part of the job description.

As we have already seen, some Jewish and Christian examples of elders who weren't necessarily old include the young prophet Daniel and the eighteen-year-old Eleazer ben Azariah, youths whose uncommon wisdom was recognized, although Eleazer's beard needed to go white overnight in order for him to be accepted by everyone as the Sanhedrin president. In the Christian tradition, about 100 CE, the bishop of Antioch, named Ignatius, wrote to the Christian community, challenging the believers to look beyond their leader's young age and to consider instead his insight and authority. "Now it is not right to presume on the youthfulness of your bishop," Ignatius wrote to the people of Magnesia in what is today Turkey. "You ought to respect him as fully as you respect the authority of God the Father. Your holy presbyters, I know, have not taken unfair advantage of his apparent youthfulness, but in their godly wisdom have deferred to him—nay, rather, not so much to him as to the Father of Jesus Christ, who is everybody's bishop."[7]

Medieval nuns and monks deferred to a person's authority, insight, and experience regardless of that individual's chronological age. The guiding document for medieval monasteries and convents was written about 530 CE by Benedict of Nursia, whom we met a moment ago. Although in the translated passages we will now consider, the masculine words *abbot* and *monks* are used, the standard procedures applied equally to abbesses and nuns in convents. In his *Rule*, Benedict discusses how monks and nuns should make decisions. It is important to note that he does not deny the voice of youth.

> Whenever any matter of moment is to be debated in the monastery, the abbot is to assemble the whole community, and to lay open the business before them: and after having heard their opinions, and maturely debated with himself, he may resolve on what he judges most profitable.
>
> We have for this reason ordained that the whole community shall be assembled, because God often reveals what is best to the young.

A few lines further, Benedict directs that for mundane matters, the abbot "is only to consult the elders," but we wonder whether these elders were older or not. In fact, as we explore further, we discover that in medieval monasteries and convents, as with ancient bodies of elders in Jewish and polytheistic societies, age was not necessarily a factor in deciding who should be a leader, adviser, or elder. We see this dynamic at work when Benedict discusses what specific places (*precedences*, to use the proper term) older and younger members should take at prayer in the monastery, at table in the refectory, at consultation in the chapter house, and at work in the fields, kitchens, or scriptoria.

> Their places in the monastery shall be determined by their time of entry, the goodness of their life, and the decision of the abbot....
>
> According to the precedence which he has determined, or which they observe amongst themselves, they shall go to the kiss of peace, receive the Holy Communion, lead the Psalms, and take their place in the choir. Wherever they are, age shall be neither here nor there

in determining precedences; for Samuel and Daniel, though but children, were made judges of elders.[8]

It is evident that a certain respect is being paid by juniors to seniors, but it appears that these are relative words. A junior might be an older person who has just recently joined the monastery or convent, while a senior could be in her thirties but prominent because she has been a member of the convent since childhood. The key sentence from the passage we just cited must be "Their places in the monastery shall be determined by their time of entry, the goodness of their life, and the decision of the abbot" — the same custom that Buddhist monasteries had been following for centuries already. *Junior* and *senior* referred, then, not necessarily to the number of years a person has been alive, but to the number of years a person has been at work and prayer in the monastery or convent.

Given this formula, the next passage from Benedict's *Rule* would indicate that those who are further along on the spiritual path, despite their age, deserve respect from others who are just starting out, also despite their age.

> The junior monks are to honor the seniors, and the seniors to love the juniors. In talking to one another, no one may call another by his own name. But the seniors shall call the juniors "brothers," and the juniors shall call the seniors "Reverend fathers."...
>
> Wherever the brothers meet, the junior shall ask the senior's blessing. When the senior passes by, the younger shall rise to give up his seat; and he shall not presume to sit down again till he is bidden by the senior.

Perhaps the most important example of this dichotomy between age and authority comes in Benedict's important rule for electing an

abbot or abbess. He says that the whole community should unani-
mously elect a person but, barring that possibility, everyone should
agree with the candidate that "a part of the community, though a
minority, has chosen with greater prudence."[9] Benedict's way of pro-
ceeding and taking counsel based on experience and not age was
cited for centuries by a Latin formula, *maior et sanior pars*, which
can be translated as the "greater and weightier part." *Maior* gives us
the word *major*. *Sanior* is related to the word *senior*, of course, but
here it means more seniority or experience than a greater number of
physical years of life, as in today's category of "senior citizens."

Throughout the Middle Ages, we find a diverse group of
communities claiming this phrase, *maior et sanior pars*, to argue
that either a majority vote wins or a small group of smarter electors
can make a more informed, sounder decision for everyone else.
They have more *gravitas*, or weight, than others. Monks and nuns
continued to use the phrase, but so did communities of scholars
and students in medieval universities starting in the twelfth century
as well as tradesmen forming guilds and city fathers called *burghers*
as they wrote their new town charters. Priests will claim that they
can elect their own bishops, and then cardinals and popes use the
principle to set up election rules in papal conclaves, sweeping aside
unanimous votes in favor of the more logical, reasonable, and practical majority of two-thirds of those voting. These are all examples
of the *maior et sanior pars* in action.

A Heart Open to Wisdom

For our purposes, what binds all of these examples together
is that age does not appear to be the deciding factor in whether
particular people have the wisdom necessary to make good decisions. Joshua, for example, is one of those biblical characters
described as old and advanced, or full of years. We read that he
dies at the age of 110, although a later commentary tradition said
he made it to 120—one of those special numbers reserved for

sages. But the Christian theologian Origen, writing from Alexandria or Caesarea in the early third century, said that it wasn't Joshua's age that made him stand out. Origen followed our now-familiar riff on the word *elder* to make his point in a learned homily on the Book of Joshua: "In Scripture, the name of elder or old man is not given because of great age, but is granted in order to honor maturity of judgement and gravity of life, especially when the words 'full of days' are added to the term 'elder.'" Maybe Benedict had read Origen when he was thinking about his plan for the *maior or sanior pars* in monasteries and convents.

In a similar way, the fourth-century Christian bishop and theologian John Chrysostom repeated a point that Jewish and pagan cultures had made: white hair may well indicate a life lived well by the virtues. "Honor to white hair, not that we have a predilection for this color, but because it is the color of virtue, and because this venerable exterior leads us to conjecture that the inner man also has white hair." In his very next breath, however, John Chrysostom warned that an old man who has lived by the vices can be nothing but a pitiable fool despite the fact that he has survived many years. As John Chrysostom put it, "But the old man who gives the lie to his white hair by his behavior, is only the more ridiculous."[10]

As we've noted, the Bible plays with the very idea of age in places, indicating that old age is not necessarily a chronological state, but a way of life or a stage of enlightenment. Consider this passage from the Book of Wisdom:

> For the age that is honorable comes not with the passing
>   of time,
>   nor can it be measured in terms of years.
> Rather, understanding is the hoary crown for men,
>   and an unsullied life, the attainment of old age.
>
>   (Wis 4:8–9)

Here, it appears that white or gray hair has become a metaphor for old age in place of a pile of years, and an untainted life is standing in for a ripe old age. We have, then, a contrast with the following passage from Sirach, which we examined earlier in this chapter:

> How becoming to the gray-haired is judgment,
>> and a knowledge of counsel to those on in years!
> How becoming to the aged is wisdom,
>> understanding and prudence to the venerable!
> The crown of old men is wide experience;
>> their glory, the fear of the Lord.
>
> (Sir 25:4–6)

In this passage, we read a clear connection between chronological old age ("those on in years"; "aged"; "old men") and rewards: judgment, sound counsel, understanding, prudence, wide experience, and glory.

Is this difficult to reconcile? Certainly, but we can look at this apparent contradiction as another rich and humbling example of the paradoxes that have become a hallmark of this exploration about wisdom. The paradox should not confound us, but rather intrigue and lead us to greater perceptions and insight of a complicated, sophisticated reality in both biblical times and our own.

That reality seems to be that, young or old, the key to pleasing God and gaining wisdom is to follow God's plan and "to see as God sees," as Pope Francis said. Based on the word *understanding* in these two passages from Wisdom and Sirach, let's explore another passage from Psalms, noting especially how it uses the word *understand* as a noun and a verb:

> Oh, how I love your law!
>> It is my meditation all day long.
> Your commandment makes me wiser than my enemies,
>> for it is always with me.

I have more understanding than all my teachers,
    for your decrees are my meditation.
I understand more than the aged,
    for I keep your precepts....
Through your precepts I get understanding;
    therefore I hate every false way.
(Ps 119:97–100, 104)

Understanding, then, is the key to a full life—be it a life of many years or a life of however many years, as long as those years are lived according to virtue and God's way of doing things.

So wisdom may not come with age and, in a reversal, a young person like Elihu can have wisdom despite having lived only a few decades. An instructive passage comes from Ecclesiastes 4:13: "Better is a poor but wise youth than an old but foolish king, who will no longer take advice." Why is the old king foolish? Because he won't take advice, which likely means either that he was never wise in the first place, despite his age, or that he is no longer wise because he's stopped learning or even being open to the idea that he still has anything to learn. A passage from Deuteronomy decrees that a king must have a written copy of the laws, which:

> shall remain with him and he shall read in it all the days of his life, so that he may learn to fear the LORD his God, diligently observing all the words of this law and these statutes, neither exalting himself above other members of the community nor turning aside from the commandment, either to the right or to the left, so that he and his descendants may reign long over his kingdom in Israel. (Deut 17:19–20)

The lesson seems to be that although a man is wise, old, and a king, he should realize that he still needs to seek and take advice—

which would be evidence not only of the virtue of wisdom, but of humility, too.

An old person, king or not, must be open to humility by realizing that many years don't necessarily bring the fullness of wisdom. As the rabbis put it, what matters is not the container, but the wine: the older the wine, the deeper the flavor—and by metaphorical extension, the greater the wisdom. *Pirke Avot*, part of Talmud from which we've drawn several times, taught, "He who learns from the young, to what is he like? To one who eats unripe grapes, and drinks fresh wine from his vat. But one who studies from the old, to what is he like? To one who eats ripe grapes and drinks old wine." In another passage, the rabbis direct us to "look not on the jar but on what is in it; there may be a new jar that is full of old wine / and an old one in which is not even new wine." We see here the typical metaphor that there is clearly something good in being old—in this case, aged wine—but that old jars or well-aged wineskins don't necessarily contain the best vintage.[11] In other words, while the word *old* follows a cultural presumption that wisdom is necessarily tied with advanced age, this presumption can be more metaphorical than actual. We have seen this with Daniel and Eleazer ben Azariah, younger monks or nuns, and youthful bishops who were considered old wine in young skins or jars.

Recognizing Wisdom, Honoring Our Elders

We continue to encounter paradoxes: Should we honor our elders because they are wiser? What if they are older but not wise? There is a Talmud story about a certain Rabbi Meir, who said he would stand up in the presence of an old man even if he knew the aged fellow was ignorant because "the very fact that he has grown old must be due to some merit."[12] But others thought that not every old person should be honored simply because of age. By contrast, for example, Rashi taught that we should not automatically revere an old person based simply on long life. Rashi spent his career in France and Germany, dying at the age of sixty-five in 1105. His commentaries were well-known. It's especially important to note that he was writing for a wide audience with the goal of providing devotional material to the masses. What he had to say had quite an impact.

Treating the important and common biblical command concerning old folks, "You shall rise before the aged, and defer to the old" (Lev 19:32), Rashi did not drop into pious platitudes or cheap slogans. Instead, he very carefully pointed out the meaning of words: "From the first part of the verse one might infer that one should stand up even for an uncultured aged person! Hence Scripture, in the second part of the verse, says *zaken* ('old man'), with the connotation of 'one who has acquired wisdom.' How does one 'honor' an old man? One should not sit in his place or contradict his words." For Rashi, a person must be old *and* wise before he'll give up his seat.

Another translation of this same verse in both the Bible and in Rashi's commentary on the passage might make the case even more strongly and tie in with our study of the word *elder*. "You shall rise in the presence of an old person and you shall honor the presence of an elder" (Lev 19:32). In this second translation, Rashi's interpretation appears this way: "One might be able to think that his commandment applies even to a condemnable elder. To teach us otherwise, the verse says, 'an elder.' 'An elder' implies only one who has acquired wisdom." Regardless of which translation we prefer—and the helpful use of the word *elder* in the second does fit in neatly with what we've been exploring so far—our next logical question would be: So what was wisdom in Rashi's eyes? The answer, according to other things Rashi wrote, is to know Torah, presumably by studying *midrashim* like that written by Rashi himself. Otherwise, a condemnable elder is "an old person who is wicked and ignorant," specifically "one who is ignorant in Torah."[13]

Other cultures agreed that an old person without wisdom is not worthy of respect and may even be deemed marginal, a failure, or disposable. The Chinese sage, Confucius (ca. 551–479 BCE), curtly dismissed those who lived to an old age without remaining active and useful. We read in his *Analects*, "The Master said, Those who when young show no respect to their elders achieve nothing worth mentioning when they grow up," making us first think that he agrees with the Talmud's Rabbi Meir that we should stand up for every old person every time we encounter one. But there's an important payoff coming next for Confucius: "And merely to live on, getting older and older, is to be a useless pest."

Again, it is the quality of a life that matters and not the quantity of years a person has amassed, as is clear from a collection of Buddhist poems called the *Dhammapada* from the third or second century BCE. There, we read that "a man is not old and venerable because gray hairs are upon his head. If a man is old only in years then he is indeed old in vain. But a man is a venerable 'elder' if he is in truth free from sin, and if in him there is truth and righteousness, non-violence, moderation, and self-control."[14]

In late medieval France, Christine de Pizan chided old women who didn't learn from experience. In her *The Treasure of the City of Ladies*, also known as *The Book of the Three Virtues* (1405), she concedes that old folks are often said to be wiser than the young because of greater understanding based on broader experiences. But de Pizan immediately adds a critical disclaimer:

> So therefore, they are likely to be wiser, and if they are not, they are the more reprehensible. Inevitably nothing is more ridiculous than old people who lack good judgement or who are foolish or commit the follies

that youth prompts in the young (and which are reprehensible even in them). For this reason the elderly
woman ought to see to it that she does nothing that
looks foolish.

What might this admonition to avoid looking foolish mean,
specifically? De Pizan notes,

> It is seemly for any older woman to be sensible in her
> actions, her clothing, facial expression and speech….It
> is not seemly for her to dance, frolic about or to laugh
> uproariously. But if she is of a happy disposition (as
> some people are, more than others, and there is noth-
> ing wrong with that), she ought always to see that she
> takes her pleasure sedately and not in the manner of
> young people, but in a more dignified way.

Here, then, is less a celebration of a medieval woman's wisdom
than a societal custom of putting her in her place. She can be
wise and dispense wisdom, but she must not make a show of it;
she must remain humble about the act of being old and wise.
At the same time, it's quite possible that the old woman has not
learned from experience at all and so remains foolish, prompting
de Pizan to call her ridiculous and reprehensible. That's quite a
striking statement in any period and from any author, let alone
a female voice who herself broke her community's glass ceiling
by supporting herself, a widow with three children, as a writer.
Maybe it was her own achievement that caused de Pizan to be
angry with other, less successful women who had not triumphed
over difficult circumstances.

She urged young people to aid the elderly with charity,
albeit in the context of the harsh verdict, "for there is no worse
disease than old age." Our medieval author directed young people to seek out only those seniors who are indeed wise and to obey

them with the recognition that these older folks had what the young did not.

> It is to your advantage to abide by the judgement of wise elderly people more than by your own and to make use of their advice and be governed and ruled by them in your most important undertakings....For in spite of the great strength of the young, if it were not for the wise elderly people the world would be in chaos. Holy Scripture bears witness to this very thing, saying, "Woe betide the land of which the king or lord is a child," that is, immature [Eccl 10:16].

A few lines further, de Pizan reiterates the point that not every old person possesses wisdom, a statement that should humble her older readers as well as warn her younger audience.

> But to get back to our subject, the teaching for women: elderly people possess the above-mentioned good sense and advantages, that is, those men and women who are honourable and wise, for we do not mean some unfortunate old people hardened in their sins and vices, in whom there is no sense or goodness whatsoever. These people are to be avoided more than any other living thing, but any young woman who desires honour ought to make friends gladly with the good and respectable ones and happily go to feasts or whatever place in their company, more so than with young women, for she will be more praised for it and she will gain more self-confidence.[15]

De Pizan's ambivalence—or should we say, deep biblical insight—has much to teach us about age, wisdom, and humility. We have learned that one of God's greatest gifts is wisdom. We are learning that this gift might come from long experience and culminate in old age or it might be granted in a *kairos* flash to a young person. We've learned, too, that humility can be closely related to wisdom at whatever stage of our lives the lessons are learned and the gifts granted. As a passage of *midrash* states, "There is an old age without the glory of long life; and there is long life without the ornament of age. Perfect is that old age which has both."[16]

Chapter 4

Let's Make
a Deal, God

Children who grow up knowing their grandparents often get a daily dose of advice from someone with far more experience. In fact, it becomes noticeable that the older some people get, the more likely that they'll say just about anything to just about anybody. "You look fat in that" or "That's a dumb idea" may sound harsh, but professionals who serve the elderly will be quick to tell the rest of us, "Older people lose their filter." Let's see this approach in a positive light, however. They have a longer perspective and aren't afraid to leverage their experience by bargaining, advising, cajoling, and telling it like it is because they know what's right and what's wrong. *That's* wisdom.

BLESSINGS AND CURSES

A very stark example of a biblical character who sees and tells it like it is can be found in Jacob at the end of his life. This is another example of a biblical episode few have heard or read. In

Genesis 49, Jacob is 147 years old and now living in Egypt. His favorite son, Joseph, brought him there after reconciling with the brothers who had sold him into slavery many years before. Sensing his own end is near, which turns out to be true, Jacob calls around himself his twelve sons. They may be expecting sage advice and a loving farewell, maybe even a nice inheritance. Instead, Jacob hits most of them right between the eyes with the wisdom and insight he's gained about each of their personalities.

Reuben is up first. As firstborn, he must be excited and expecting to be given a very large portion of Jacob's inheritance. Instead, Jacob tells Reuben that he is unstable and will never be excellent. Next up: Simeon and Levi. Jacob curses them both for their violence and hopes never to be in their company again, although he praises Judah, Zebulun, and Issachar for their strength, courage, and hard work. Dan is a judge, but also a dangerous viper; Gad will both raid and be raided. Asher will enjoy rich food and Naphtali "is a doe let loose that bears lovely fawns" (whatever that means). The favorite, Joseph, not surprisingly, comes in for exceptional praise, while Benjamin is dismissed as "a ravenous wolf." Some of these words sound strange and harsh, but for Jacob, they were nevertheless truthful.

In fact, as you read the Bible, it's easy to miss these unexpected lessons and gifts, as we have seen already with Elihu in the story of Job and see here again with Jacob. If you pause and read carefully, so as not to overlook small incidents and to take for granted larger ones, it will not take long to notice that the more experienced some people become, the more insightful and bolder they get, just like Jacob in this scene of blessings and curses. In addition, the biblical school of hard knocks endows some biblical characters with the ability to bargain with God as well as with a deep perspective. Abraham and Moses, two of the most revered biblical figures, are not afraid to stand toe-to-toe with God. They negotiate, nudging God again and again as they gain some ground each time.

We also find a great deal of perspective that allows some biblical characters to weather storms with calm. They have the ability to wait troubles out because they have learned that God's sense of time is often not the same as ours. We think of the patient Abraham and Sarah in Genesis and their Christian gospel counterparts, Zechariah and Elizabeth. Each couple has a child when the chance for such things is normally long past. There is also the obscure Barzillai who has the guts and sense of himself to turn down a king's offer of a leisurely retirement. Finally, there is Naomi, a very savvy lady working behind the scenes to make things turn out just the right way.

BARGAINING, PERSPECTIVE, AND SELF-AWARENESS

Abraham and Moses

Maybe the best known story of biblical bargaining is when Abraham continually banters with God to rethink the decision to destroy Sodom and Gomorrah (Gen 18:16–19:29). What Abraham is trying to do is save the lives of his nephew, Lot, and his family. We can calculate Abraham to be about one hundred years old at this point. Whether he has actually hit the century mark or not, whether that age is a metaphor or a fact, it's clear he's an old man at this time. His long experience is part of what makes him bold and courageous enough to bargain with God.

To set the scene: God decides that Sodom and Gomorrah are so corrupt that the only solution is to wipe the two cities out. Abraham, fearing for his nephew, asks God a logical question: "Will you indeed sweep away the righteous with the wicked?" It's not just a factual question, but something of a philosophical dilemma, like wondering why bad things—such as car crashes, hurricanes, and earthquakes—happen to good people. Abraham really pushes God to wonder if the presence of fifty righteous folks could spare the city, cajoling the Lord: "Far be it from you to do such a thing, to slay the righteous with the wicked, so that the righteous fare as the wicked! Far be that from you! Shall not the Judge of all the earth do what is just?" And so God relents, saying that if Abraham can find fifty good people, Sodom would be spared.

It turns out that fifty was just Abraham's opening bid. Maybe he feared he couldn't find so many, so he knocks the number down to forty-five and God agrees that forty-five will do. But Abraham is just getting started, successfully winnowing God down to forty righteous people. Fearing that he's overplaying his hand, Abraham continues: "Oh do not let the Lord be angry if I speak. Suppose thirty are found there?" Once more, God relents, and Abraham keeps going: what about twenty? OK, says God, but Abraham's not yet done. Knowing he's probably pushing his luck, once again Abraham begs God's indulgence: "Oh do not let the Lord be angry if I speak just once more. Suppose ten are found there?" The deal is done: if Abraham finds ten righteous men in Sodom, God will not destroy the city.

We know the rest: there aren't even ten righteous people, so God levels the city and countryside with a rainstorm of sulphur and fire. Thanks to some angels, who give Lot and his family a warning and then drag them out of their house when they hesitate, Lot and his two daughters are spared. His wife could have survived, too, but she doesn't take the angels' warning not to look back. She turns to see the disaster and is transformed into a pillar of salt. Abraham looks sadly over the burning, smoky scene the next morning, perhaps fearing for Lot and his family because it's clear the patriarch couldn't find even ten righteous men to save the city. Still, "God remembered Abraham, and sent Lot out of the midst of the overthrow." Lot is now a widower, but he has his two daughters in tow, thanks to the brave badgering of an old man with his God.

Another story that comes not from the Bible but Islamic tradition tells us that Abraham was bold enough to bargain with God about when he would die, too. Genesis indicates that Abraham is 175 when he "breathed his last and died in a good old age, an old man and full of years" (Gen 25:7–8). Much later, the eleventh-century Islamic source called *Lives of the Prophets* says that Abraham "had once asked his Lord to let him die when he himself would ask to die." According to this story, when he was 195 or 200 (other versions have him at 175 or the very precise 194), Abraham saw a frail old man off in the distance. Ever the hospitable host, Abraham sends a donkey so the old man doesn't have to walk. When he arrives, Abraham offers him food, which the visitor mistakenly puts in his eye and ear before finding his mouth. As soon as he swallows the food, it comes right out of his rectum. Abraham asks the old man why this happened, to which he replies simply: "Abraham, it is old age." Abraham asks just how old his guest is.

> When he told him, Abraham made a calculation and found that the man's age exceeded his own by only two years. Abraham said to him, "There are only two years between us, and when I reach your age, shall I be like you?" He said, "Yes." So Abraham said, "God take me before that!" The old man arose and took Abraham's soul, for the old man was the Angel of Death.[1]

Apparently, if Abraham can't eat well, he doesn't want to live — and so God grants the faithful Abraham the ability to pick his own time for a happy death, escaping some of old age's physical breakdowns.

Moses, too, isn't afraid to speak boldly to God. He is already about eighty when he encounters God at the burning bush. Even though God is on his side, Moses often seems to be trying to get out of doing things because he's scared or overwhelmed—and he's clearly not afraid to say so. When God orders Moses to speak to Pharaoh, Moses wonders whether the great king will listen to a "nobody" like him. He wonders if he's even up to the task, wondering aloud to God, "Who am I that I should go to Pharaoh, and bring the Israelites out of Egypt?" (Exod 3:11). Moses tells God that he has never been eloquent. He pleads, "O my Lord, please send someone else," which is how Aaron, his elder brother by three years, ends up as Moses' spokesman (Exod 4:10–17).

As we follow Moses, time and again we find rather unheroic behavior: complaining, whining, pestering, and fretting. The Yiddish word *kvetch* best describes Moses' bargaining with God.[2] Moses can come across as weak, fearful, and faithless. He laments that God is being harsh to the Israelites and himself: "O Lord, why have you mistreated this people? Why did you ever send me?…You have done nothing at all to deliver your people" (Exod 5:22–23). But here is also a wise man of bravery, surely borne from his experience, who is not afraid to bargain and negotiate with God. Once he sees results, Moses starts telling God what to do: the plagues of frogs and flies did their job, the patriarch informs the Lord, so you can get rid of them now (Exod 8:12–13, 30–31). The *kvetching* seems to be working.

Emboldened by God and his own success, Moses gains courage. He now has the strength to speak more truth to power in his audiences with Pharaoh. When the Egyptian ruler permits the Israelites to sacrifice, but only on Egyptian land, Moses informs him that they will do so in the desert wilderness far from Egyptian eyes (Exod 8:25–29). Pharaoh gives in partially, allowing the men to worship, but Moses says everyone must go—men, women, children, and livestock—and the Lord sends locusts and darkness as a threat (Exod 10:7–29).

As time passes, the ever bolder Moses bargains more with God and even changes the divine mind. Furious that Aaron has made a golden calf and the Israelites have turned away from their deliverer, the Lord wants to punish them. Moses cautions God not to give the Egyptians a chance to say, "See, God wanted to kill them after all." Put more bluntly, Moses warns God not to be a liar, since God has promised Abraham, Isaac, and Jacob the Promised Land and a long line of descendants. "Turn from your fierce wrath," Moses tells God forcefully and directly, "change your mind" (Exod 32:12). God listens: "And the LORD changed his mind about the disaster that he planned to bring on his people" (Exod 32:14).

This story of the golden calf is famous, although usually not so much for Moses' boldness as to point out how short memories and gratitude can be. But for our investigation into biblical wisdom, there are three other, lesser known stories about Moses tucked away in the Book of Numbers. All three show him bargaining, negotiating, and cajoling with God. He may have been loath to talk to Pharaoh, but it's not long before Moses is completely unafraid to take God on, reminding us of Abraham playing poker with God to save Lot. Perhaps that is because we tend to think of Moses and Yahweh in a kind of friendship whereas Moses and Pharaoh were adversaries. Maybe Moses learned that it is easier to cajole friends than enemies.

The first story appears in Numbers 11 at a stage in the Exodus story where Moses is clearly exhausted and fed up not only with the people he's leading, but also with the Lord. The Israelites are in the desert when they tire of the manna God provided so they could survive. They want meat. God gets mad at the people, and Moses gets mad at God:

Then the LORD became very angry, and Moses was dis-
pleased. So Moses said to the LORD, "Why have you
treated your servant so badly? Why have I not found
favor in your sight, that you lay the burden of all this
people on me?…Where am I to get meat to give to all
this people? For they come weeping to me and say,
'Give us meat to eat!' I am not able to carry all this
people alone, for they are too heavy for me. If this is
the way you are going to treat me, put me to death at
once—if I have found favor in your sight—and do not
let me see my misery." (Num 11:10–15)[3]

God responds precisely and readily to Moses' complaint by telling
him to set up a council of seventy elders to help bear his burden.
And yet, Moses is still audacious and exasperated enough to keep
at it, telling God that he has six thousand mouths to feed, but
cannot figure out how God can fulfill a pledge to keep them full
of meat for a month since there is hardly any space for large herds
or a sea full of fish around them. It's at this point that God says
the biblical equivalent of "Oh, yeah?" in an exchange that reads
like an argument between two cranky but still loving friends. "Is
the LORD's power limited?" God asks Moses rhetorically. "Now
you shall see whether my word will come true for you or not." At
this point, God sends flock after flock of quails so the people will
not starve.

The second story is found in Numbers 14, where once more
we find Moses negotiating with an angry God. The people are
grumbling again. Despite their prior bondage in Egypt, that's
exactly where they want to return. God is once again annoyed by
their short memories and ingratitude, so a pestilence as punishment seems to be in order. Moses intervenes at this point, calm-
ing God down and telling the Lord that the divine reputation is
still at stake. In what reads like an appeal to God's vanity (if such

a thing could exist), Moses says, "Now if you kill this people all at one time, then the nations who have heard about you will say, 'It is because the LORD was not able to bring this people into the land he swore to give them that he has slaughtered them in the wilderness'" (vv. 15–16). Moses mentions Yahweh's reputation as merciful and just, then commands—not asks, *commands*— "Forgive the iniquity of this people according to the greatness of your steadfast love, just as you have pardoned this people, from Egypt even until now" (v. 19). What happens? God does just that, forgiving the people because of Moses' cajoling.

Our third example of bargaining power comes at the end of Moses' life in Numbers 27 and Deuteronomy 3—two chapters that go together. At 120 years old, Moses figures his time is coming soon, saying elsewhere, "I am no longer able to get about" (Deut 31:2), although unlike Isaac and Jacob, his eyesight notably does not fail. God informed Moses that he would see the Promised Land, but not cross over into the land of Canaan himself. Moses pleads for a successor to be named in his lifetime. This is an important teaching moment pointed out by rabbis of the early third century CE that is included in their collected wisdom sayings called the Tannaitic Commentaries. Given this particular exchange between God and Moses, these rabbinic commentators drew the following lesson: "If Moses, the wisest of the wise, the greatest of the great, the father of prophets, knowing that a decree had been made against him, nevertheless did not refrain from asking for mercy, certainly others should not!"[4]

What other lessons might modern readers draw from Moses' persistence, especially at the end of his own life? Two major insights come to mind. First, Moses realizes that he will not live forever; he is in touch with his own mortality and bears no illusions. Second, he knows that naming a successor will allow him time to train the new leader, to give him some advice, and to ensure a smooth transition instead of a power struggle after his own death, which means that Moses' own mission will continue. Moses makes a wise decision, and tells God to appoint a successor—Joshua—while he's still alive.

Unlike many arrogant and narcissistic leaders, Moses knows that the world will go on without him, but he also knows there are ways to shape his legacy before he is gone. He's not one of those people who may secretly wish that the whole enterprise will fall apart after his own death, proving that he was after all superior and indispensable—not unlike how many historians read the death of Alexander the Great in 323 BCE. Alexander refused to name a successor, on his deathbed answering the question of who should receive his throne and the vast areas he had conquered with the enigmatic: "to the best."[5] What Alexander lacked at the end of his short life of 33 years, and what Moses possessed at the end of his long life of 120 years, was perspective. Alexander didn't want anyone to carry on his work for fear the successor would surpass him. Moses, on the other hand, was aware of his own weaknesses. He knew he needed a successor so his own life's work would continue as his legacy after his death. Who is the wiser leader?

Barzillai

Barzillai the Gileadite provides another instance of perspective and open eyes with no delusions at the end of a long life. In an obscure, short scene in 2 Samuel 19:31–39, we meet Barzillai, who is depicted as a worn-out eighty-year-old. The only other place in the Bible where Barzillai appears is a brief reference when he helps David and his retinue by providing them with food as they flee from Absalom.

Years later he's visiting David, now king, in Jerusalem. David, mindful of Barzillai's help all those years ago and respectful of his old age, asks him to stay comfortably in the capital.

Barzillai doesn't even consider the offer, asking with what we imagine to be a bemused, self-aware, and reflective tone,

> How many years have I still to live, that I should go up with the king to Jerusalem? Today I am eighty years old; can I discern what is pleasant and what is not? Can your servant taste what he eats or what he drinks? Can I still listen to the voice of singing men and singing women? Why then should your servant be an added burden to my lord the king? Your servant will go a little way over the Jordan with the king. Why should the king recompense me with such a reward? Please let your servant return, so that I may die in my own town, near the graves of my father and my mother. (2 Sam 19:34–37)

You can just hear Barzillai saying, "Really? Come on!" King David graciously relents, gives Barzillai a kiss of peace, and sends him off. We last see Barzillai on his way home, surely to die in his own bed and to be buried with his parents, a man at peace with his life and death.

Curiously, the eleventh-century rabbi Rashi, commenting on this text, notes that *midrashim* did not praise Barzillai. Rashi quotes an earlier commentary, which interpreted Barzillai's response to David in these terms:

> If you seek my presence in Jerusalem because you desire my counsel, I can no longer adequately discern between good and bad. If, on the other hand, you do not seek my advice, but desire only to recompense me by providing me with the luxuries of palace life, can I, at my age, yet taste etc.?

Another rabbi speculates that the ability to discern between good and bad refers to the appreciation of good food rather than to dispensing sound advice or moral judgement. Rashi quotes the Talmud, "Now our rabbis have stated that he was highly promiscuous and therefore aged rapidly." Here, Maimonides, the twelfth-century Spanish rabbi who lived just after Rashi, states his opinion "that excessive promiscuity is a major cause of aging and curtailment of life."

These assessments take us back to some initial biblical notions that a long life is a reward for virtue and service; therefore, a short life is the punishment for vice. Furthermore, if it is the case that Barzillai's taste buds no longer function well, then he reminds us of Abraham, who would rather enjoy his food than expel it as soon as it passes his lips. Indeed, Rashi cites the Talmud's example in the commentary alongside of a ninety-three-year-old maidservant who still enjoys the taste of food by way of contrast.[6] Despite what Rashi and other commentators have said, however, it remains true that whether he was a good man or bad, he just wants a quiet place to rest and to die at home. He doesn't want to cut any deals with David except to be left alone. Barzillai enjoys the wise perspective and clear-eyed self-awareness that experience has brought him. He's not fooling anyone, least of all himself. Barzillai knows who he is.

Naomi

We find these same types of bargaining, perspective, and self-awareness in the short and moving Book of Ruth. For our purposes, the star of the story is not the title character, Ruth, which is how this book is normally read. Our journey focuses on a widow named Naomi, who is too old to have a husband. She has two adult sons who died and is close to her daughter-in-law, Ruth. Naomi doesn't want to be a burden: she tries to dismiss her daughters-in-law, seeing herself as someone who has fallen out of favor with God. "No, my daughters, it has been far more bitter for me than for you, because the hand of the LORD has turned against me" (1:13). When Naomi and Ruth arrive in Bethlehem looking for food, some old acquaintances there think they recognize her. They ask if she is, indeed, Naomi, a name that means *pleasant*. But hungry, worn-out, and maybe even desperate, Naomi tells them to call her Mara, meaning *bitter*, "for the Almighty has dealt bitterly with me" (1:20).

But from this low point in her life and the story, Naomi's prospects pick up—and she's wise enough to recognize a potential change in fortune. This is when the perspective of her hard years comes into play, a perspective that makes her see a negotiating opportunity when it arises. Naomi notices that a man named Boaz, a relative of her late husband, has taken a liking to Ruth, sending Naomi into "Yente-the-Matchmaker" mode. Naomi gives Ruth advice on attracting Boaz's attention because, as the mother-in-law tells Ruth, "My daughter, I need to seek some security for you, so that it may be well with you" (3:1). Dress up and look sharp, Naomi says, but do not let him know who you are until the right moment. Boaz finds himself quite impressed with Ruth's character, especially her devotion to the older Naomi.

Boaz marries Ruth, receiving land and property tied to Naomi's dead husband and two sons, and carrying on the dead man's name. In due time, Ruth and Boaz have their own son, Obed. When her friends hear of Obed's birth, they shout with joy to Naomi, "Blessed be the LORD, who has not left you this day without next-of-kin" (4:14). They even proclaim, "A son has been born to Naomi" (4:17), instead of to Ruth, the boy's biological mother. Naomi's friends rejoice that she now has someone to care for her: "He shall be to you a restorer of life and a nourisher of your old age" (4:15). We imagine Naomi delighting in her role, late in life, as Grandma. Moreover, her impact on Obed is considerable and historic. Obed will be the father of Jesse, whose son is David, making Naomi the great-great-grandmother-in-law of one of the greatest Hebrew heroes in the Bible. None of this would have taken place had Naomi not had the courage and moxie to wisely switch from a passive victim of hard, bitter times into an active player in her own life, a switch born out of difficult times that nearly—but ultimately didn't—defeat her.

We can add a wonderful example of these virtues from pagan sources dating to biblical times. When the Greek philosopher Plato wrote his *Republic* in the fourth century BCE, he included an encounter between his own mentor Socrates and Socrates's elderly friend, Cephalus, now living a comfortable retirement something akin to what Barzillai wanted. Cephalus's candid portrait of his later years attracts our attention.

Socrates visits Cephalus at the pleasant port town of Piraeus, Athens's supply line to the Aegean Sea. Cephalus, "seated on a cushioned chair and crowned with a wreath," describes the fact that as bodily pleasures have faded and he finds himself freed from lusts of the flesh, he enjoys using his mind more, especially in lively discussions. Socrates replies that he enjoys speaking to very old people, from whom he can learn how to travel the path of life, daring to ask Cephalus specifically what it's like to be old since "your foot is on the threshold." The old man replies that he and his friends like to get together and talk. We all reminisce and some complain or miss carousing, Cephalus relates, while others "keep harping on old age as responsible for all their troubles."

But I love being old, Cephalus says, and the issue is not really his age, after all, but having a sense of who you are and what your character is. "If one is well-ordered and content, even old age is but a moderate burden," he tells Socrates. Old age is a time for reflection.

But rest assured, Socrates, that when someone begins to face the thought that he is going to die, there comes upon him a troubled fear about things that never used to worry him before. The stories told about the place of the dead, and how those who did injustice here must suffer justice there, were once ridiculous; but now they torture his soul for fear they may be true. And he himself—either from the weakness of old age, or perhaps because he is as it were closer now to the things beyond and sees them somewhat more clearly—however it may be, he is filled with fearful second thoughts, and begins to cast up accounts and consider whether he has ever done any injustice to anyone. Well, if he finds numerous injustices in his own life, he wakes often even from sound sleep in fear as children do, and lives with foreboding; but in him whose conscience finds nothing unjust, hope is ever present to cheer him, a kindly nurse to old age.[7]

All of these stories—the bargaining Abraham and Moses, the cantankerous Jacob, the seemingly minor characters Barzillai and Naomi, and the ancient pagan Greek Cephalus, too—remind us of the power of the Greek phrase, "Know thyself," which was carved into Apollo's temple at Delphi and is also attributed to Socrates. To know who you are with no delusions is clearly a step toward wisdom in the ancient world, whether you were a polytheistic pagan or a Hebrew monotheist. This self-awareness reveals a special type of biblical wisdom, since you can only make a good deal when you know what cards you're holding.

Chapter 5

Blessings and Burdens

ENJOYING BLESSINGS

The psalmist uses a phrase we hear in many cultures throughout history: "May you see your children's children" (Ps 128:6). May we be blessed to be grandparents for "grandchildren are the crown of the aged" (Prov 17:6). Job is rewarded for his faithfulness: he lives to see four generations after his own. But the Bible tells us we need not live quite that long, making the century mark a metaphor during darkness and a prophecy of a new creation in better times, as in Isaiah 65:20:

> No more shall there be…
>> an old person who does not live out a lifetime;
> for one who dies at a hundred years will be considered a
>> youth,
>> and one who falls short of a hundred will be considered
>> accursed.

God promises blessing and reward for a lifetime of service and obedience. As the years pass, a person's stature would rise; God was blessing a righteous person with long life and wisdom. As Proverbs says, "A ruler who lacks understanding is a cruel oppressor; / but one who hates unjust gain will enjoy a long life" (28:16). Earning a few more years may also indicate that God is pleased with our prayers. Hezekiah, king of Judah (ca. 715–687 BCE), was deathly ill and asked God to help him: "Remember now, O Lord, I implore you, how I have walked before you in faithfulness with a whole heart, and have done what is good in your sight." Maybe Hezekiah had learned something from Abraham or Moses on bargaining with God (or perhaps he'd read the previous chapter). Yahweh seemed to recognize the truth of what Hezekiah said and granted him fifteen more years to live (2 Kgs 20:1–6/Isa 38:1–6).

The Bible shares this general notion that age is a mark of divine blessing with the rest of the ancient Near East culture in which it was written. A hymn dating from the seventh century BCE tells us that the Mesopotamian god of the sun and justice named Shamash rewards upright judges who turn back bribes and protect the poor: "As for him who declines a present but nevertheless takes the part of the weak, it is pleasing to Shamash and he will prolong his life." According to Babylonian wisdom literature, it is the honest merchant who pleases the gods and so prolongs his life—a gift given by Shamash not only to judges in high places, apparently, but to working-class sellers in the market, too. A number of Hebrew Scripture passages agree that if you don't cheat, you'll live long. "You shall have only a full and honest weight; you shall have only a full and honest measure, so that your days may be long in the land that the Lord your God is giving you" (Deut 25:15).[1] If a butcher didn't tip the scales in his own favor, God would be sure to tip the scales to favor the butcher.

Let's return briefly to that well-known commandment to honor our fathers and mothers. As we noted in an earlier chapter, a lesser known nudge follows those famous words: "So that your days may be long in the land that the LORD your God is giving you." There are a few insights about blessings gained from this one familiar rule of honoring our parents that can be easily over-looked and misunderstood. First, our parents are worthy of our respect; second, it is possible that the young are not, in fact, hon-oring their parents properly, which is why God has to lay the deed down as law; third, honoring our parents might be the right thing to do, but children and grandchildren need some incentive: their own extended lives and good reputations as respectful children; and fourth, that very fact—that the children and grandchildren's reward is long life—tells us that long life is, indeed, regarded as a blessing for virtuous behavior.

Rashi, the medieval French rabbi who has already fallen into step with us several times on this journey into biblical wis-dom, found a clear interpretation to this journey. Honor your par-ents and your life will lengthen; fail to honor them and your life will shorten. Akkadian literature from early biblical times indi-cates a similar assessment: "A man who does not fear his father will perish quickly." Mesopotamia's *Code of Hammurabi* from about the eighteenth century BCE dictates that "if a man strikes his father, they shall cut off his forehand." Another legal text of that time directs, "A son who says: 'You are not my Father,' shave his head, put the mark of a slave on him and sell him. A son who says to his mother: 'You are not my mother!' Shave half of his head and lead him round the city and put him out of the house."[2]

Time and again, the right relationship between generations is commanded in the Bible. If a person strikes or just curses his father or mother, he will be killed (Exod 21:15, 17; Lev 20:9). We even get a vivid scene of how it will play out:

> If someone has a stubborn and rebellious son who will
> not obey his father and mother, who does not heed

them when they discipline him, then his father and his mother shall take hold of him and bring him out to the elders of his town at the gate of that place. They shall say to the elders of his town, "This son of ours is stubborn and rebellious. He will not obey us. He is a glutton and a drunkard." Then all the men of the town shall stone him to death. So you shall purge the evil from your midst; and all Israel will hear, and be afraid. (Deut 21:18–21)

Though some of these passages do not speak directly of old age, logic dictates they are referring to rules concerning senior citizens. Sometimes, the connection is explicit: "Listen to your father who begot you, and do not despise your mother when she is old" (Prov 23:22). After the fifth commandment, the next most-quoted biblical passage on our topic, and one we have encountered already, is "You shall rise before the aged, and defer to the old" (Lev 19:32). In other translations, this comes out as "You shall rise before the hoary head," indicating someone with white or gray hair or maybe an older person with a weathered look or wizened demeanor.

Other ancient cultures made at least a face-saving attempt to honor the elderly, too. We noted that the Spartans allowed twenty-eight men over sixty to serve on the powerful *Gerousia* in their government, indicating a large measure of respect for quite old men, given this historical period and the fact that we are talking about a warrior society. Word of the Spartans' manner of honoring their elderly got around. Several hundred years after Sparta's peak, the Roman orator and statesman, Cicero, wrote a treatise on old age called *De senectute* in 45 or 44 BCE. Being in his early sixties and winding down his career in law and politics, Cicero tells a terrific story of an old man entering an Athenian theatre. He looked for a seat but not one Athenian stood up so the old man could sit. He must have given up hope, but then he reached the section where the visiting Spartans (normally the Athenians' rivals and even archenemies) were sitting. When the old man got to the Spartan section, every single Spartan stood up to offer his place. The entire audience applauded. "These Athenians know what politeness is," one of the Spartans observed, we imagine with a sneer, "but they won't practice it."[3]

So popular and well-known was this story that, over fourteen hundred years later, the medieval French author Christine de Pizan (ca. 1365–1429) included a slightly different version of it in her handbook *The Treasure of the City of Ladies*, or *The Book of the Three Virtues* in a section titled, "How young women ought to conduct themselves towards their elders." After retelling Cicero's story of the old man and the Spartans, de Pizan then instructed, "You children and young people should take this example to heart as a sound doctrine, for you should know that Right and Reason want to have honor accorded to them, and even Holy Scripture bears witness to this." Following the Bible, de Pizan made the point that honoring the elderly is not only right in itself, but would bring its own rewards, as both versions of the famous fifth commandment nudged (Exod 20:12; Deut 5:16). As she put it:

> You may be certain that you will be greatly praised for doing this, for honor does not reside with the person to whom it is done but with the one who does it. And if you owe honor to the elderly, it follows that at all costs you must avoid mocking them and doing or saying injurious, derisive or outrageous things, or bad things of whatever kind. Do not displease or find fault with them, as some wicked young people do who are very much to be reproached for it, who call them "old boys" or "old biddies"; this is a clear reproach to one who otherwise conducts herself well.[4]

Exactly why God rewarded some biblical people with long life and not others is not always clear; some were clearly faithful, but all naturally had human flaws, as well. One of the keys to God blessing particular biblical figures with long life seems to be their desire to live well and be virtuous, as we saw with Hezekiah. When Solomon prays for wisdom, God answers, "If you will walk in my ways, keeping my statutes and commandments, as your father David walked, then I will lengthen your life" (1 Kgs 3:14). We don't find a precise age for David at his death: "When David was old and full of days" he turned his reign over to his son Solomon, dying "in a good old age, full of days" (1 Chr 23:1; 29:28). Calculating a few passages reveals that David most likely was at least seventy, since we're told he was made king at the age of thirty and reigned for forty years (2 Sam 5:4). Interestingly, we do not have an age of death for the wise king Solomon, who according to tradition had a dialogue with God recorded in the Book of Proverbs. Specifically, we find there several passages that support the idea that long life is God's blessing for virtuous living:

> My child, do not forget my teaching,
>   but let your heart keep my commandments;
> for length of days and years of life
>   and abundant welfare they will give you.
>   (Prov 3:1–2)

> Hear, my child, and accept my words,
>   that the years of your life may be many.
>   (Prov 4:10)

> The fear of the LORD prolongs life,
>   but the years of the wicked will be short.
>   (Prov 10:27)

The psalmist, too, promises long life as a reward, particularly in one passage that has been a consolation to people suffering and in sorrow for many centuries and around the world:

> Those who love me, I will deliver;
>> I will protect those who know my name.
> When they call to me, I will answer them;
>> I will be with them in trouble,
>> I will rescue them and honor them.
> With long life I will satisfy them,
>> and show them my salvation.
>
> (Ps 91:14–16)

There is no guarantee, of course, that old age always means a glorious end or even signifies a worthwhile long life. We all know grumpy, miserable people who never seem to go away. Still, it seems clear that most of the time old age is God's blessing for good behavior. In Deuteronomy 30:19–20, for example, we read that we should "choose life so that you and your descendants may live, loving the LORD your God, obeying him, and holding fast to him; for that means life to you and length of days." Proving the point, we also have, by way of an exception, the sons of Eli. Their father, Eli, was a good priest at Shiloh and the prophet Samuel's mentor, but his sons were wicked. A man is sent by God to Eli, a bit of a sad figure at this time, and tells him, "See, a time is coming when I will cut off your strength and the strength of your ancestor's family, so that no one in your family will live to old age…and no one in your family shall ever live to old age" (1 Sam 2:31–32). A blessing can be given as well as held back—or perhaps Yahweh didn't want those wicked sons to have too much time to cause trouble.

QUANTITY VERSUS QUALITY

We might ask, however, about the quality of an old person's life in the Bible. There is old age, of course, but what will it be like? Would we want to live to 120 if our last 30 years were full of suffering and we couldn't get around?[5] At the very end of his life, Moses still has good eyesight and energy. And we have the model of Caleb, a deputy to Moses who kept God's commandments faithfully and scouted out the Promised Land when he was forty. Now at the age of eighty-five, Caleb tells Moses' successor, Joshua, with pride, "I am still as strong today as I was on the day that Moses sent me; my strength now is as my strength was then, for war, and for going and coming" (Josh 14:11).

It is a delightful discovery to find that, as many women get older in the Bible, their worth and blessings often rise. In the ancient and medieval world, older women played an important, nearly mystical role as midwives standing between life and death. Their trade was especially important for widows and postmenopausal women who needed a source of income and a place of standing in society now that they'd passed childbearing years.

A little-known offstage episode to a famous biblical tale of Moses' birth tells the story (see Exod 1:15–22). Egypt's Pharaoh summons two Hebrew midwives, named Shiphrah and Puah, and orders them to kill all newborn Hebrew boys. Instead of following orders, they completely ignore Pharaoh's command, so he angrily summons them again: "Why have you done this, and allowed the boys to live?" Pharaoh demands. The midwives wisely choose to obey God rather than man. They lie straight to Pharaoh's face: "Because the Hebrew women are not like the Egyptian women; for they are vigorous and give birth before the midwife comes to them." God, it seems, was quite pleased: because of the midwives' bravery, God's people grew in number and strength. "And because the midwives feared God," the story concludes, "he

gave them families." Wise, strong, and likely postmenopausal—
like Sarah before them—the older women Shiphrah and Puah
were honored, rewarded, and blessed by God.

We have other evidence that a woman's value and role as a
sage rose as she aged. With female mortality higher than men's
because of the dangers of childbirth, a woman who lived a long
time was naturally seen as strong in body and soul. The Book of
Leviticus, a precise legalistic text early in the Bible, specifies the
value of men and women at certain ages by indicating the payment
to be made in place of a particular vow, fine, or service. Notably,
the worth of women rises in real and relative value over time, as a
close look at this chart adapted from Leviticus 27:1–8 indicates:

Age	Male	Female
1 month– 5 years old	5 silver shekels	3 silver shekels
5–20 years	20	10
20–60 years	50	30
60+ years	15	10

A girl from age five to twenty years old is worth just half what a
boy is worth, but her value rises as she ages. Instead of her prior
value as half a man, a woman is worth 60 percent of a man when
they are both in the prime of their lives (20–60 years old). It's
depressing to find that a man's worth drops off so sharply: he loses
70 percent of his value when he turns sixty years old. By contrast,
an older woman's value at sixty years old increases comparatively
to two-thirds of a man's, even though her practical value plummets
from thirty shekels down to just ten.

Notice that relative to a man's value, an older woman in the
Bible is worth more now than ever before in her preteen through

adult life. After sixty, the woman is surely a grandmother and matriarch full of her family's history, tending a brood of grand-children and sometimes great-grandchildren, passing along her reverence for God, and praising virtuous living. Rashi considered Leviticus's comparison of male and female value, especially as both got older: "A man decreases in the sum of his valuation as he reaches old age by more than a third of his valuation, while a woman decreases by only a third of her valuations, for people say, 'If there is an old man in the house, there is something broken in the house. If there is an old woman in the house, there is a trea-sure in the house and a good sign in the house.'"[6]

We might say, then, that in traditional societies represented by biblical times, it's not unusual to discover the young depicted as vigorous and engaged while the old are sick and unable to function or, instead, moving onto a new phase of their lives where they enjoy the blessings of a life lived well. We find women, especially, transi-tioning into positions as wise and trusted arbiters, counselors, and experienced givers of advice. Plato, in his *Laws*, advised that the oldest guardians were the best people to oversee the care of orphans, which must have included women.[7] In ancient Rome, menopause gave some women greater liberty to move around: since older women were no longer able to get pregnant, the fear of unwanted pregnancy with its social stain and the problem of inheritance issues that came with bastard children ceased to be an issue. Although even older Roman women were still under the custom-ary rule of *paterfamilias*, the legal authority of a male that in some cases might even be an old mother's young son, their prestige and influence rose as they became grandmothers.[8] And so women, especially, were revered as keepers of wisdom.

EMBRACING BURDENS

Along with many inspiring biblical passages and stories identifying long life as God's blessing for faithful service and virtue, we also find a fair number of lamentations. There is simply no way around the truth that aging can be a rough path, one full of physical infirmity, emotional pain, sadness, and abandonment. In our attempt to tell a full story, we must also embrace this biblical paradox. Age can be a reward, yes, but it was also clearly a burden, even a curse in some cases. We begin with the obvious physical toll that hard work and poor medical care took on aging bodies throughout the ancient and medieval world, and even into modernity, which has had the good fortune of penicillin for less than a century—barely a minute in the long history of human life, disease, and death.

The Bible doesn't shy away from the damage that advancing years rain down on a person. The physical manifestations are clear. We hear that the priest Eli is "very old" and his "eyesight had begun to grow dim so that he could not see" (1 Sam 2:22, 3:2). It turns out he is ninety-eight, "an old man, and heavy." Eli died after falling backward over his chair and breaking his neck when he learned that the Philistines had taken the Ark of the Covenant in battle (1 Sam 4:15–18)—an ancient version, perhaps, of the debilitating broken hip that is often feared as a slippery slope toward life as a shut-in today. The mighty prophet Samuel refers to himself as "old and gray" (1 Sam 12:2), though we're not given a number for his age. Rashi's commentary quotes an earlier tradition that Samuel lived to fifty-two but had aged prematurely, perhaps because he prayed that God would take him before King Saul died. So God aged Samuel prematurely to conceal the fact that he died "at an early age," as this rabbinic commentary put it. Apparently, dying at the age of fifty-two was premature, and God was sparing Samuel from the physical woes of old age.[9] Eyesight also failed the minor, mostly unknown prophet Ahijah, whose eyes had grown sightless with age, an affliction that often applied to better-known figures such as Eli.

Isaac, in a far more well-known story with an overlooked detail that concerns us here, is tricked because of his old eyes. Isaac, we read in Genesis 27, "was old and his eyes were dim so that he could not see," maybe suffering from glaucoma or cataracts. Thinking he might be at the end of his life (though he ends up living another twenty years), Isaac summons his son Esau and asks him to prepare food, after which Isaac will bless him. Isaac's wife, Rebekah, plays favorites between their twin sons Esau and Jacob. Esau had been born a moment before Jacob and, as the older brother, was supposed to be heir. But Rebekah overheard Isaac and helped Jacob beat Esau to the punch. Jacob brings in a meal that Rebekah had cooked. Jacob is wearing Esau's clothes and some animal skins to fool their father.

Isaac has a sense that something is not quite right. "Come near, that I may feel you, my son, to know whether you are really my son Esau or not," Isaac says, even asking Jacob directly, "Are you really my son Esau?" Jacob comes close and Isaac, nearly blind, gives him a sniff. "Ah, the smell of my son," meaning Esau, the outdoorsy twin. Isaac, fooled, blesses Jacob as Esau. Being tricked once is bad enough, but Isaac is betrayed yet again a few passages later. Rebekah, fearing that the furious Esau will kill Jacob because of the stolen blessing, contrives to send Jacob away to safety, but then she tells Isaac a different story. Rebekah convinces Isaac to tell Jacob to leave and marry a distant relative, so that Jacob's escape is, in Isaac's mind at least, a plan for his prosperity. We now have not only eyesight as a burden of old age, but a sense of confusion, too. In his older years, Isaac seems to be played as a fool and taken advantage of not once, but twice, by his wife and child.

We find an epilogue to this story later, in Genesis 48, when Jacob himself is now old. The episode is thick with irony for the aged Jacob, who is described as having eyes "dim with age, and he could not see well," just like his father Isaac all those years ago. Jacob's son, Joseph, was by this time a powerful man in Egypt, having been sold as a slave by his brothers because of Jacob's favoritism toward Joseph. Jacob asks Joseph to bring his two sons, Ephraim and Manasseh, forward for a blessing from their revered grandfather, the family's patriarch.

Jacob breaks protocol and places his right or favored hand on Ephraim, the younger son, and his left on Manasseh, the older boy. Joseph is annoyed, maybe flabbergasted, by what he takes to be his old father's confusion. He tries to move Jacob's hands to the more traditional position: right hand on the older Manasseh and left on the younger Ephraim. Jacob will have none of it. We imagine Jacob is recalling his own treachery against Esau when he says stubbornly to Joseph, "I know, my son, I know; [Manasseh] also shall become a people, and he also shall be great. Nevertheless his younger brother shall be greater than he, and his offspring shall become a multitude of nations." Old and nearly blind, it's important to Jacob that he is in control of the situation, as his father Isaac had not been, and to be the player and not the one being played. Perhaps, in fact, it was his physical sightlessness that gave Jacob insight in his mind's eye.

We also find that biblical men must move away from physical tasks as they age. The Book of Numbers, like Leviticus with its sometimes-numbing set of rules, singles out in detail three clans of men whose work is directly related to the tent of meeting, which is the traveling tabernacle that houses the Ark of the Covenant. The age for this work is set precisely at thirty to fifty years old—physically and psychologically mature enough to do the job, but not so old that they might drop a precious object. The Kohathites' job is to carry the tent's furnishings and adornments, although

they may not look at or touch them. Once packed, the adornments are to be hoisted onto the Kohathites' shoulders. The
Gershonites carry the inner structures of the tent, such as
screens, cords, and curtains. The Merarites carry the tent itself:
frame, poles, pegs, and other parts of the structure. All three
clans are related to the priestly Levites, a prestigious fourth group
of men who undertake their assigned work between the ages of
twenty-five and fifty years old. Levites begin their duties five years
younger than the other groups' starting eligibility of thirty years
old, likely because their tasks are a bit less physical since they
perform liturgical rituals within the tent.

It's clear from this careful delineation of ages and tasks in
Numbers 4 that the assigned jobs are physically strenuous, since
they are called there "the work of bearing burdens." At age fifty,
the men from all four groups are forced to retire; by implication,
those over fifty are considered unable to carry out adequately the
tasks of packing, carrying, and setting up the tent and its pieces,
inside and out. Rashi commented that men are too weak before
thirty and after fifty to do their assigned labor. "But one who is less
than thirty, his strength has not become fully developed....And
one who is more than the age of fifty, his strength diminishes from
then on."[10] What an emotional burden it must have been for
men, some perhaps still strong, to be told that—like it or not,
ready or not—their fiftieth birthday was time to end their careers,
a Biblical mandatory retirement age that could not have been fair
or logical in every case. Surely all remained proud of their faithful
service and enjoyed a level of prestige in their homes and circles
in addition to a well-deserved rest. But for others not yet ready to
stop working (then and now), forced retirement must have been a
weight heavier than the packs they'd carried for twenty years.

A loss of mental capacity matches the loss of physical ability,
too. In 1 Kings 11, we find the famously wise king Solomon who
gets hoodwinked by his wives at the end of his own long life. Here

is a cautionary tale about one of the burdens of old age: a diminished sense of judgment that makes an elderly person vulnerable to manipulation, like the episode of Isaac's stolen blessing. As this story goes, Solomon's foreign wives turn him away from Yahweh, for whom the king has built that glorious temple in Jerusalem. God has warned the Israelites not to marry women from certain foreign lands specifically because "they will surely incline your heart to follow their gods." This is precisely what happens to Solomon; the poor old king was made a fool for love many times it seems, given his seven hundred princesses and three hundred concubines.

> For when Solomon was old, his wives turned away his heart after other gods; and his heart was not true to the LORD his God, as was the heart of his father David. For Solomon followed Astarte the goddess of the Sidonians, and Milcom the abomination of the Ammonites. So Solomon did what was evil in the sight of the LORD, and did not completely follow the LORD, as his father David had done. Then Solomon built a high place for Chemosh the abomination of Moab, and for Molech the abomination of the Ammonites, on the mountain east of Jerusalem. He did the same for all his foreign wives, who offered incense and sacrificed to their gods. (1 Kgs 11:4–8)

Not surprisingly, God is pretty angry, especially since he has twice appeared to Solomon to warn him against this very thing happening. In retribution, God tells the old king that he will take away his immense kingdom. But in deference to Solomon's father David, God says he will wait until Solomon's reign is over and take the kingdom away from his son, although even then God says he will leave the family one tribe. It is a King Lear-like moment from the Bible: the wily king, reduced in his dotage to misjudgments, is taken advantage of by those less worthy than he used to be. It's interesting that this episode with such important results is largely unknown or overlooked. Because the episode reflects so poorly on wise Solomon, we may wonder if tradition simply pushed this uncomfortable story into a closet, making it a hidden tale. Regardless, it is one that can still teach us a lesson today.

Yet again, we are faced with a biblical paradox: age does not by its very nature always lead to reverence or prestige. Respect for old age had to be enforced in the face of disrespect, if only so that ancient folks might feel good about themselves when they talked about how they treated their elders. In the period when the Old Testament was concluding and the New Testament was starting, about 100 BCE–200 CE, the Romans believed that old age was not necessarily a blessing or a burden. Romans in the late Republic and early empire of these centuries saw old folks as being remarkable because of achievements in their youth. Some may have been honored not because of their age, therefore, but in spite of it. One study of old age among the Romans asserts in words depressing to modern ears that elderly Romans were "not... full members of society." Part of the problem is that most literature from the period is written by and about aristocrats rhapsodizing about ideal images of old age—how they'd like to be viewed, which might be very different from reality.

It's possible that there are odes to old age's glories precisely because the burdens were so dominant and the respect that should have been shown to old people was evident so infrequently. Even Cicero, who generally sings the praises of age and honor in his *De senectute* written just at this time, is honest enough to admit that for the poor or rich, a wise person or a fool, aging can be a burden, too. A fool does not become a wise man worthy of pomp, praise, and protégés just because he hits a certain age. Fools, he says, assign to their old age their own faults and vices, but these were with them all along: "For an intemperate and indulgent youth delivers to old age a body all worn out." If you were wealthy like Cicero, old age offered the possibility of a graceful exit from public duties and a leisurely period to reflect on the good old days. But for most of the population of average workers from ancient times up to today, you worked until you couldn't. Retirement is not an option. If you are productive, you're valuable and appreciated. If you can't work, you and your old age with its aches, pains, and the inability to accomplish your allotted tasks become a burden not only to yourself, but also to everyone around you. At best, you might be tolerated. At worst, you could well be alienated and tossed aside.[11]

This disturbing perspective that old age was a burden did not change as the centuries passed. A distressing medieval portrait was written by an Italian lawyer and Catholic cardinal named Lothario dei Segni, his given name before he ascended to the papal throne as Pope Innocent III (1198–1216). In his thirties, just a few years before his papal election, he wrote *De miseria humane conditionis* (*On the Misery of the Human Condition*), which, despite its dour title, ended up being copied in at least seven hundred manuscripts and printed in over fifty volumes. His treatise warns that worldliness is dangerous to your soul, which was an important message at the time. Medieval Europe was just emerging from a few dim centuries, and a commercial revolution was exploding: the economy was expanding quickly and cities were growing faster. A materialistic race for money and power was on. Dei Segni, trained in theology and church law, adopted a common genre to caution entrepreneurs and those caught up in this medieval rat race, including people like himself serving in the church's highest echelons.

Using the metaphor of an old, worn-out body and mind, dei Segni advises against greed. He instructs readers that their pursuit of wealth will produce vices, especially pride, and not virtue. The destination of such a life is hell, not heaven. Surely he exaggerates to make his spiritual points: he oversells his case with a heavy admonishing hand and wagging finger. The piece may read even more harshly because of the fact that he never got to finish the work; he likely planned a counterbalancing second half on the virtue of humility, which would have softened the whole treatise and provided the payoff. In the half we have, he makes the point that no matter your health and vigor in youth, your body will break down physically in old age. More importantly, your personal qualities will decline the same way. The future pope asks, Why put your faith in the world and your body when both will pass away? A wise insight, indeed.

It is better to have contempt for the worldliness that surrounds us, although that doesn't necessarily mean becoming a cloistered nun or a monk. As with Augustine's *City of God*, written early in the fifth century, dei Segni wants people to live according to God's rules while engaged in this world in order to prepare for the next. He warns that, at some point, both the world and your own body will ultimately betray you, no matter how powerful or rich you are:

> If anyone does reach old age, his heart weakens, his head shakes, his vigor wanes, his breath reeks, his face is wrinkled and his back bent, his eyes grow dim and his joints weak, his nose runs, his hair falls out, his hand trembles and he makes silly gestures, his teeth decay, and his ears get stopped with wax.

At this point, dei Segni goes on to describe the decline of a person's behavior, demeanor, and mental capacity that accompanies the body's frailties. It is a grumpy, gullible old man that our author presents as an object lesson.

> An old man is easily provoked and hard to calm down. He will believe anything and question nothing. He is

stingy and greedy, gloomy, querulous, quick to speak, slow to listen, though by no means slow to anger. He praises the good old days and hates the present, curses modern times, lauds the past, sighs and frets, falls into a stupor, and gets sick.

And then we have the lesson by way of caveat:

> But then the old cannot glory over the young any more than the young can scorn the old. For we are what they once were; and some day we will be what they are now.

One scholar has noted that dei Segni, a cardinal in the Roman curia at this point, was working under a very old pope and likely describing what he observed of one of the most powerful human beings on earth at the time. In fact, Pope Celestine III was the oldest man in history to be elected pope, chosen at the age of eighty-five in 1191. About seven years later, around Christmas, a weak and tired Celestine suggested to his cardinals that he might abdicate the papal throne on condition that he would name his successor. The cardinals refused and he stayed on, but Celestine died just a few weeks later at the age of ninety-three — a feat matched by only one other pope in history so far: Leo XIII died at almost ninety-three-and-a-half in 1903. As it turned out, Celestine III's favored candidate lost in the papal election that followed in 1198, and dei Segni was elected Innocent III. The young had succeeded the old, although Innocent III would die before he turned sixty.[12]

A similar perspective can be found in a short book of wisdom literature in the Bible known as Ecclesiastes. Its author is called the Preacher, or Qoheleth, who is usually linked with Solomon. Although it's unlikely Solomon is the book's author, not least of all because it was probably written about five hundred years after he died, the passages carry the weight of his reputation for wisdom.

In a now-familiar lesson and one that Cicero would also share a few hundred years later, the author tells us that it is not the quantity of a human life that matters, but its quality. "A man may beget a hundred children, and live many years; but however many are the days of his years, if he does not enjoy life's good things, or has no burial, I say that a stillborn child is better off than he" (Eccl 6:3).

Ecclesiastes contrasts youth with old age near its conclusion, providing a warning to both the young and the elderly. "Rejoice, young man, while you are young, and let your heart cheer you in the days of your youth," the Preacher says. "Follow the inclination of your heart and the desire of your eyes, but know that for all these things God will bring you into judgment" (Eccl 11:9). He proceeds to tell young people that they must always look ahead:

> Remember your creator in the days of your youth, before the days of trouble come, and the years draw near when you will say, "I have no pleasure in them"; before the sun and the light and the moon and the stars are darkened and the clouds return with the rain; in the day when the guards of the house tremble, and the strong men are bent, and the women who grind cease working because they are few, and those who look through the windows see dimly; when the doors on the street are shut, and the sound of the grinding is low, and one rises up at the sound of a bird, and all the daughters of song are brought low; when one is afraid of heights, and terrors are in the road; the almond tree blossoms, the grasshopper drags itself along and desire fails; because all must go to their eternal home, and the mourners will go about the streets; before the silver

cord is snapped, and the golden bowl is broken, and the pitcher is broken at the fountain, and the wheel broken at the cistern, and the dust returns to the earth as it was, and the breath returns to God who gave it. (Eccl 12:1–7)

While discouraging, Qoheleth's message is enlightening in that it uses the metaphor (actually, a number of metaphors jumbled together) of old age as a caution to young people, demonstrating yet again how much old age, though it could be characterized by honor and respect, is in the end more often full of heavy burdens, no matter how successful a person has been in his or her youth. Not for nothing does the book end where it begins, with the famous refrain "Vanity of vanities, says the Teacher, vanity of vanities! All is vanity."

And yet, in some of his very last words, the author gives us an appealing peek into his own tasks (Eccl 12:9–10, 12). "Besides being wise, the Teacher also taught the people knowledge, weighing and studying and arranging many proverbs. The Teacher sought to find pleasing words, and he wrote words of truth plainly." The job, it seems, wore him out in the end. "Of making many books there is no end," the Teacher wrote, "and much study is a weariness of the flesh." We, at least, can be blessed by gathering wise insights from the burdens of his old age.

Chapter 6

Patience and Humor

Patience, we are told (usually by our exasperated parents), is a virtue. The Bible offers three examples of men and women whose chance to be parents is behind them. We imagine they have waited many heartbreaking years to be parents. For whatever reasons, they have not been blessed with children; yet in their later years, the older women find their patience has paid off with a pregnancy. The reaction is amazement, to be sure, and of course joy, but also laughter. As parents and grandparents in every era and of any age know, patience and a sense of humor are good to have when raising children.

In the Bible, we find infertility in older men as well as post-menopausal women. A woman past menopause cannot, of course, become pregnant and give birth, but then we have Sarah's pregnancy with Isaac at age ninety and Elizabeth's pregnancy with John the Baptist at an advanced, though unspecific, age. Even in a world before Viagra, a man's age does not necessarily limit his ability to impregnate a woman. Abraham is eighty-six when Hagar gives birth to their son, Ishmael, and ninety-nine when Sarah becomes pregnant. Zechariah is advanced in years like his wife,

Elizabeth. In another overlooked anecdote, the prophet Elisha promises a Shunammite woman who has cared for him that she will have a son, even though her husband is old (2 Kgs 4:14–17). These are miracle stories and by definition out of the ordinary. Yet the stories of Sarah and Abraham, Elizabeth and Zechariah, and the Shunammite husband and wife make an important point about the patience that comes with age. We can learn a valuable lesson from the wisdom of these biblical characters.

The first story is nothing new to our ears. Abram is seventy-five when he first hears God's call. God promises that he'll be buried in that prototypical "good old age." But he's childless in his mid-eighties until his wife Sarai offers her Egyptian slave-girl Hagar to Abram. Hagar and Abram have a boy named Ishmael. Then, God makes a covenant with the ninety-nine-year-old Abram, who is circumcised as a sign of this covenant and whose name is now changed to Abraham. At that time, when Sarai is ninety, she hears that she will give birth to a boy named Isaac and her name becomes Sarah.

When they learn that she is pregnant, both Abraham and Sarah burst out laughing. We read that Abraham is so taken aback that he "fell on his face and laughed, and said to himself, 'Can a child be born to a man who is a hundred years old? Can Sarah, who is ninety years old, bear a child?'" (Gen 17:17). Overhearing three mysterious visitors telling Abraham that his wife will have a son, she chuckles to herself, "After I have grown old, and my husband is old, shall I have pleasure?" And then there's a delicious exchange where Sarah, suddenly frightened, denies laughing, at which God replies, "Oh yes, you did laugh" (Gen 18:9–15). Apparently, you can't fool God.

Curiously, Genesis twice mentions Sarah bearing Abraham a child "in his old age" instead of hers, but it is notable that the first time in the Bible that we hear mention of a woman's age it is to identify Sarah as 127 at her death. Our medieval rabbinic commentator Rashi specifically praised Sarah for being as sinless at one hundred as she was at twenty: "Just as one who is twenty years old is considered as if she has not sinned, for she is not liable to punishment, so, too, when Sarah was a hundred years old she was without sin. And when she was twenty years old she was like seven years old with regard to beauty." Rashi, in turn, was working off an earlier rabbinic commentary that read, "The complexion of a seven-year-old is more beautiful than that of a twenty-year-old. Alternatively, women tend to become increasingly more beautiful from the age of seven to the age of twenty, when they attain the height of their beauty. Sarah's beauty continued to develop at the age of twenty at the rate of a seven-year-old." For Abraham's part, Rashi says that when he was a hundred, he was like seventy, and "when he was seventy years old he was like five years old, without sin."[1] Ishmael and Isaac, it turns out, are not to be Abraham's only children. Often overlooked, once he got started at eighty-six and after Sarah died, Abraham remarries somewhere in his late 130s and with this second wife, Keturah, has six more children.

In the first of our two overlooked anecdotes, we hear little more of the old Shunammite husband and his wife except for one telling episode that indicates how much we should appreciate the gifts we receive, especially late in life (2 Kgs 4:18–37). The old fellow and his wife unexpectedly have a son just as Elisha had predicted. Working in a field with his father one morning, this boy complains of a headache and dies on his mother's lap at noon. She lays him on a bed that Elisha used when visiting, then sets off resolutely to find the prophet, telling her husband that she needs a servant and a donkey to get going quickly. When the husband tells her to wait, she won't be stopped. She orders her servant, "Urge the animal on; do not hold back for me unless I tell you." Locating Elisha, she grabs his feet and won't be set aside. Elisha sends his own servant ahead to try to revive the boy, but the

Shunammite woman insists that Elisha come himself: "As the LORD lives, and as you yourself live, I will not leave without you." The prophet can't resist and sets off with her. When he arrives, Elisha raises the boy from the dead. We're told in striking detail how it happens: "The child sneezed seven times, and the child opened his eyes." Once she had that little boy with her aged husband, there is no way she is going to take this gift of the boy's life for granted. Patience had led to the boy's birth and persistence brought him back to life.

Our final story comes from Christian Scripture (Luke 1:5–20). A priest named Zechariah is married to Elizabeth. "Both were getting on in years," we're told. One day, while Zechariah is offering incense in the Lord's sanctuary, he is terrified by the appearance of an angel. The angel tells Zechariah that he and his wife will have a son, but the priest doubts what he hears. "How will I know that this is so? For I am an old man, and my wife is getting on in years." The angel, who is Gabriel, then informs Zechariah that because he doubted, he will be struck mute until the birth. Elizabeth suddenly conceives this child, a pregnancy she then hides for five months.

This is the normal time for confinement culturally, perhaps, but there is an interesting interpretation of this story found in the medieval collection of saints' lives called the *Golden Legend*. Around the year 1260, a Dominican preacher named Jacobus de Voragine compiled these stories in order to demonstrate how the saints' lives reveal God's presence and help in salvation history. We read in his collection of tales that a fourth-century bishop of Milan named Ambrose speculated that Elizabeth may have "felt some shame at having a child at her age, fearing that she might seem to have indulged in lustful pleasure despite her years." Maybe Elizabeth, like Sarah so many centuries before, thought that her sexual activity might be considered unseemly by nosy neighbors. No matter, as the *Golden Legend* continues, Elizabeth "also rejoiced at being rid of the reproach of sterility. It is a source of shame for women not to have the reward that belongs to marriage, since it is in view of that reward that marriage is a happy event and that carnal union is justified."[2] Elizabeth shares her joy with her cousin Mary, a very young girl at the opposite end of life who also found herself suddenly and mysteriously pregnant. When that same angel, Gabriel, appeared to Mary six months later, the young girl's fears were calmed by the angel's announcement that "your relative Elizabeth in her old age has also conceived a son" (Luke 1:36).

We find a lovely coda and lesson of patience in these three pregnancy stories. Here we are dealing not with older folks who have a child themselves, but a man and a woman who rejoice and delight at the news of a child's birth, like the joy Naomi and her friends felt when Ruth and Boaz had Obed. Perhaps this is a promising message for some seniors who think they'll never have grandchildren.

The characters of Anna and Simeon are not blood relations to Mary or Joseph, but they play an important role in Jesus' story in Luke 2:25–38. Simeon is not given an age, but we know that he is waiting for his death, which God told him wouldn't occur until he'd seen the Messiah. Luke describes Simeon as "righteous and devout, looking forward to the consolation of Israel, and the Holy Spirit rested on him." On a particular day, that Spirit led Simeon to the Temple, where he saw Mary, Joseph, and Jesus. As soon as Simeon caught sight of them, he realized that Jesus was the promised Messiah. In a beautiful scene repeated in homes and hospital rooms around the world, this old man cuddled that tiny baby in his arms. "Master," Simeon told God, "now you are dismissing your servant in peace, according to your word."

Nearby stood Anna, a woman "of a great age" (eighty-four, as it turns out), who was revered as a prophet. She fasted and prayed in the Temple all the time, like so many men and women who spend much time in prayer or community service in their retirements today. Anna overheard the righteous and devout Simeon speaking with Jesus' parents. "At that moment she came, and began to praise God and to speak about the child to all who were looking for the redemption of Jerusalem."

Simeon and Anna—both senior citizens—are among the first to proclaim the belief in Jesus as the Messiah. Pope Francis played with the idea of old and young when preaching about this biblical story: "It is a meeting between young people who are full of joy in observing the Law of the Lord, and the elderly who are filled with joy for the action of the Holy Spirit. It is a unique encounter between observance and prophecy, where young people are the observers and the elderly are prophetic!"[3]

The German scripture scholar and religious reformer Martin Luther also preached on this scene from Luke's Gospel. In a sermon he delivered in 1522, Luther praised Anna as full of the Holy Spirit. Though the people around them may have dismissed Anna and Simeon as old fools, Luther stressed how prophetic, bold, and wise they were. "Now it must excite wonder that such things were proclaimed openly by Simeon in that public and sacred place with reference to that poor and insignificant child… when nothing as yet was known of Jesus." As for Anna, "full of wisdom and having a good conscience," Luther says that she "must signify those who stand by and hear this message assenting to it and applying it to themselves."[4] If we assume, surely correctly, that Simeon was of an advanced age, then some of the very first people involved in hearing about Jesus, in recognizing him as the Messiah, and in proclaiming the good news were elderly—Zechariah and Elizabeth, Simeon and Anna. It should be noted also that half were women in a world run by men.

While we aren't surprised to find the scripture professor, Martin Luther, preaching on this Gospel episode, we might not expect to find the story of a patient, old Jewish man named

Simeon resounding through the centuries and ending up in medieval Arthurian legends, yet this is precisely what happened. Simeon becomes a model for the persistent figure who protects the Holy Grail—another name traditionally applied to the cup Jesus used at the Last Supper. It is admittedly a long trail, but it begins in *Quest of the Holy Grail*, a popular retelling of the story likely written in France in the early thirteenth century, about the same time as the *Golden Legend*. In the tale of a knight named Perceval, we read that Perceval arrives in an abbey church and sees there an old man attending Mass—"a white-haired ancient, very full of years" wearing a crown, covered in wounds, clearly in pain but still alive. Perceval guesses that this old man is at least three hundred years old.

The Bible and British folklore intersect at this point. According to a British legend, Joseph of Arimathea—the man who claimed Jesus' body from the cross and buried Jesus in his own tomb—came all the way north from the Holy Land to Britain to preach the gospel. He carried with him a "precious vessel," which is always taken to be the grail. On his long journey, Joseph's son, Josephus, had converted a king called Mordrain near Jerusalem. As they traveled further, Josephus was captured by a certain Crudel. Mordrain comes to defend Josephus and kills Crudel in battle, but Mordrain is himself grievously wounded. The king prays that he might live nine generations until the one knight arrives whose personal worth allows him to see the grail (this will be Galahad). We then hear a prophecy that Mordrain will see again and that his wounds will heal.

About four hundred years pass, during which time Mordrain eats only the Eucharist, so it is that very same Mordrain whom Perceval spied during Mass at the abbey church where our story began. There, Mordrain waited like Simeon. In a specific reference to the Gospel tale, the anonymous author of *Quest of the Holy Grail* relates:

101

> From the time of Josephus to this present hour the
> king has lain waiting thus for the coming of that
> knight whom he has yearned to see: waiting as did the
> aged Simeon who watched so long for the advent of
> Our Lord that the babe was brought to the temple,
> and there the old man met him and took him in his
> arms in his joy and glee that what had been promised
> him was now fulfilled. For the Holy Ghost had made
> it known to him that he would not die until he had
> looked on Jesus Christ.[5]

Clearly, this story of the faithfulness of Simeon—similar to that of
Anna, Zechariah and Elizabeth, and Sarah and Abraham before
them—resonated through the years as a model of patience.

In conclusion, let's return to another element of Sarah's
patience—her sense of humor about her own advanced age.
Centuries after the Bible was written, the medieval Jewish sage
Maimonides considered the question with his own good humor.
"Who is an old woman?" Maimonides asked rhetorically. "One
who is called old and does not protest."[6] About two hundred years
after Maimonides, just as the Renaissance was brewing out of the
dour Late Middle Ages, the Italian humanist Petrarch wrote a letter to his friend, Boccaccio (of *Decameron* fame), on the dawn
of Petrarch's sixty-second birthday. It was July 20, 1366, and
Boccaccio was fifty-three at the time. Writing from his stance a
decade further along in life, Petrarch told Boccaccio, likely with
a chuckle, "When you feel that you are old, then and no sooner
will you declare your old age."[7]

In our own time, the Pew Research Center released a large
study called "Growing Old in America: Expectations vs. Reality."
The findings relate that most young people under the age of thirty
targeted sixty as the start of old age. But people thirty to sixty-four
years old on average pushed that number to around seventy; while

those over sixty-five years old went further to identify seventy-four as the magic number to put someone in the category of the elderly. Even then, only a third of the people over seventy-five who were surveyed said they felt old. As the survey's lead author, the Pew Research Center's Paul Taylor, put it: "There's a saying that you're never too old to feel young, and boy, have older Americans today taken that one to heart." Looking at these results, AARP's director of research, Jeffrey Love, concluded, "Old age is always a bit older than you are."[8]

Chapter 7

A Time to Reap,
A Time to Sow

There are some familiar verses that begin a beautiful biblical poem found in the Book of Ecclesiastes. It's a memorable passage that many people choose for important moments: baptisms and funerals, weddings and anniversaries, and special birthdays.

> For everything there is a season, and a time for every
> matter under heaven;
> a time to be born, and a time to die;
> a time to plant, and a time to pluck up what is planted....
> (Eccl 3:1–2)

Though these words may have been written as many as twenty-five hundred years ago, even non-Bible readers know how folk icon Pete Seeger spun these lines into his song "Turn, Turn, Turn" in the 1960s, a time of great change. Seeger chose a translation for that third line as "a time to plant, a time to reap," which of course is the standard, time-honored farming pattern: you plant seeds in spring and summer, and then you harvest grain, fruits, and vegetables in autumn to get your family through winter.

Comforting as those familiar words are, for our exploration, it's quite helpful to retranslate the phrase "a time to plant" as "a time to sow" and "a time to pluck up what is planted" as "a time to reap." Let's also flip them around: "a time to reap, a time to sow." Why? A close reading of biblical wisdom teaches us that, yes, as we would expect, old age is a time for senior citizens to enjoy the harvest of their long years of hard work and to watch their grandchildren play. Right away we'll find that the Bible presents old age as a period to relax and to pray.

Yet we can also look at the older decades as an opportunity to keep learning and even to get finally to that creative project or new field that we always meant to try but never had the free hours to take on because of family and work obligations. While the Bible advocates what we call lifelong learning—proven by every study to improve body, mind, and soul in our growing population of empty nesters—it also calls us to continue sowing, that is, to be sure to pass along the wisdom of our experience. We all know the phrase, "it's never too late to learn," but it's also never too late to keep teaching, either.

A TIME TO REAP

Take a look at synagogues, mosques, churches, and community centers and you will often notice a large number of senior citizens lending a hand. Nearly every religious service on a weekday is dominated by older men and women, which may indicate a declining membership among young people. This is a lamentable fact for some congregations, but let's be fair: it's also true that some younger and middle-aged people would like to stop and formally pray on a weekday morning, but simply can't pull it off without a very early morning service at a church, synagogue, or mosque. They've got to drop their kids off at school, rush to a meeting, catch a commuter bus or train, or get moving ahead of traffic. Retired folks, on the other hand, can more easily make it to a morning prayer service or evening Scripture study group. They have more time and greater flexibility in their schedule to help out. For many older folks, their later years become a time to reconnect with religion or to expand their involvement in their faith and community.

This is nothing new. We also find anecdotes of this kind of activity from the ancient pagan world of biblical times. In Homer's *Iliad* from about the eighth century BCE, we see a man in his prime—the warrior prince, Hector—assigning to his aged mother, Hecuba, the role she is to play as Troy fights the Greeks.

> No, mother, you are the one to pray.
> Go to Athena's shrine, the queen of plunder,
> go with offerings, gather the older noble women
> and take a robe, the largest, loveliest robe
> that you can find throughout the royal halls,
> a gift that far and away you prize most yourself,
> and spread it across the sleek-haired goddess' knees.
> Then promise to sacrifice twelve heifers in her shrine,
> yearlings never broken, if only she'll pity Troy,
> the Trojan wives and all our helpless children.[1]

While the young men fight, the older women—their mothers, in-laws, and grandmothers—turn to the gods to ask for mercy and victory. Later in time after Homer in classical Greece, even with its lip service loyalty to the elderly, we particularly find women over the age of fifty playing significant leadership roles in sacred and funeral rites. These were important tasks in a world dominated by civic religion and the critical need to sacrifice to the gods properly as well as to read their messages accurately. Plato insisted that in a perfect *polis*, the priests and priestesses should be at least sixty. Aristotle noted that the old are weary and no longer at their physical prime, which made him conclude that they are perfectly suited to serve the gods.[2]

Maybe we need to consider older age not so much as a time for slowing down as for speeding up. It's a life stage when the elderly can reap the rewards of past efforts precisely in order to branch out into new endeavors. Reaping always sounds passive — things come to you — but it can also be an active process. Given the modern world's longer lifespans, with not only more but healthier years in body and mind, retirement and old age are not necessarily tied to the end of physical abilities. As we noted earlier, in the past, a person worked until he couldn't any longer or died at his task; for women, with the physical burdens of childbearing, death at the household job was routine and expected. Today, we are better equipped to choose the timing and level of our disengagement from one field — likely the career that paid our mortgage and children's education — and our active entrance into another.

An increasing number of people now hope to retire "to" a next endeavor rather than simply "from" their first career. Some people are able financially to have two retirements, turning from one activity to another that might be less labor intensive or need not be as high-paying as the one in our younger years with their family obligations. Many seniors move from working fully in a specific field to consulting, so they can choose when, where, and how much to work. Libraries and bookstores are filled with books by older entrepreneurs offering advice on making our latter years productive. Such advice can lead to increased financial achievement, moving completely into a new field of work, or a richer and more rewarding life of study, spirituality, or volunteerism. One thing that ties all of these activities together is the ability to share experience and learned wisdom with those behind you at particular stages of their own lives and careers.

The ancient world offers examples of the elderly who earned prestige as keepers of their culture's wisdom. They reaped the rewards of status by being sought out as sages with great influence and important roles to play in their later years. For instance, Utnapishtim (meaning "I found life") is the Mesopotamian equivalent of Noah; we met him briefly in chapter 1. He functions as the elder passing along traditions to Gilgamesh, his descendant, in the classic *Epic of Gilgamesh*, dating from around the time of the Bible's earliest books. As the story goes, Gilgamesh despairs because the gods killed his friend Enkidu. So Gilgamesh goes off on a journey to find immortality. He seeks out Utnapishtim, who has been spared in a flood, earning immortality along with his wife (who is unfortunately not named). Like Noah, Utnapishtim followed the instructions of a god, in this case Ea, the god of intelligence and wisdom, and built an ark that he packed with his family and pairs of animals. Utnapishtim tells Gilgamesh a secret: at the bottom of a river is a plant that can keep a person young. The plant is called "As Old Man Becomes Child," or "As Old Man Becomes Young" in another translation. Gilgamesh finds the plant, but a snake eats it before he can. The snake gains immortality, symbolized by shedding its skin once a year. Gilgamesh knows that he can only be mortal and learns his lesson: live for today and appreciate what you have because tomorrow it may all be gone.[3]

In ancient Mesopotamian stories like this, we find a certain respect for old people, unlike the Greeks' near-total disdain and even fear of the vicissitudes of old age. One of the ways the elderly in ancient Mesopotamia (and perhaps in every place and time in history) reaped respect was by threatening to disinherit wayward or disobedient children and grandchildren. Clearly, this is an instance where seniors enjoyed the prestige that came with the recognition that they had endured many hardships and now held powerful cards in their hands. Indeed, the most common word for aging in this ancient culture is *lubburu*, translated as "to last a long time," "to live to an old age," or simply "to endure."[4]

In the ancient world, it was customary for esteemed seniors to look for examples of active elders in history as models. We meet again the Roman statesman Cicero. When he was about sixty-two, he wrote *De senectute*, his treatise on old age, and sent it to his friend Atticus, who was sixty-five. Cicero put his own observations in the mouth of Cato, who had died a century earlier in his mid-eighties. Cicero specifically had Cato point out that he kept his brain active by learning Greek at an advanced age, an example of his maxim, "Old men retain their mental faculties, provided their interest and application continue." In turn, Cato referred even further back in history to Sophocles, the fifth-century BCE playwright, who was still producing quality work at the age of eighty, as Cato's recounting of a family lawsuit testifies:

> Sophocles composed tragedies to extreme old age; and when, because of his absorption in literary work, he was thought to be neglecting his business affairs, his sons [hauled] him into court in order to secure a verdict removing him from the control of his property on the ground of imbecility, under a law similar to ours, whereby it is customary to restrain heads of families from wasting their estates. Thereupon, it is said, the old man read to the jury his play, *Oedipus at Colonus*, which he had just written and was revising, and inquired: "Does that poem seem to you to be the work of an imbecile?" When he had finished he was acquitted by the verdict of the jury.

A moment later, Cicero has Cato offering yet another model from Greek history that fascinated the Romans so much. Cato presents Solon, an Athenian lawgiver who died in the sixth century BCE, another example of an elderly man still reaping the rewards of an active mind as long as he exercises his intellect:

> But you see how old age, so far from being feeble and inactive, is even busy and is always doing and effecting something—that is to say, something of the same nature in each case as were the pursuits of earlier years. And what of those who even go on adding to their store of knowledge? Such was the case with Solon, whom we see boasting in his verses that he grows old learning something every day.[5]

About a century later, in much the same way as Cicero, the Roman philosopher and playwright Seneca wrote his *Letters from a Stoic*. Seneca was about seventy years old and had recently fallen out of his favored position as an advisor to the emperor Nero. As a portrait of a time to reap, Seneca's work echoes what Cephalus from an earlier chapter and Cato had just said. The years pass and the body's abilities and desires decline, it is true, but in their place a sense of peace, satisfaction, and reward increases in compensation. Seneca declared,

> Well, we should cherish old age and enjoy it. It is full of pleasure if you know how to use it. Fruit tastes more delicious just when its season is ending. The charms of youth are at their greatest at the time of its passing. It is the final glass which pleases the inveterate drinker, the one that sets the crowning touch on his intoxication and sends him off into oblivion. Every pleasure defers till its last its greatest delights.

What a joy it is, Seneca goes on, like Cephalus had, not to be bogged down in youthful lusts:

The time of life which offers the greatest delight is the age that sees the downward movement—not the steep decline—already begun; and in my opinion even the age that stands on the brink has pleasures of its own—or else the very fact of not experiencing the want of any pleasures takes their place. How nice it is to have outworn one's desires and left them behind![6]

Pagan philosophers weren't the only ones enjoying their retirement. Jerome, the well-trained if somewhat cranky Roman who served the pope and then went off to Bethlehem in the late fourth century to translate the Bible into Latin, noted, like Cephalus and Seneca, that while desire drops over time, wisdom can increase. "If men have trained their youth in honorable accomplishments and day and night have meditated on the Lord's law," Jerome wrote, then old age "becomes more learned by time, more subtle by experience, more wise by lapse of years and reaps the sweet fruit of its ancient studies."[7]

Experience, it seems, brings with it the chance for greater self-control and self-discipline, which is quite different from the rash and impulsive nature of young people. To make the case, we return to a notion of the ages of man as linked to the ages of the world, which we explored briefly in the first chapter. There are many examples, but let's follow the little-known Petrus Berchorius, who died in 1362. He wrote a work on morality while witnessing poor examples of Christian behavior at the papal court in Avignon. Drawing on standard ancient and medieval interpretations from thinkers like Augustine and Isidore of Seville, Berchorius believed that a human being's seven states of life reflected a path of seven spiritual virtues. The sixth state, in which the body's vigor frequently fails, he labeled *senectus*, a Latin word affiliated with wisdom and the Roman senate. But for him this failure is a *good* thing since youth's impetuous and reckless side has by now been tamed. In this sixth state of life, a person's spirit reaps insight (*prudentia*). This Benedictine monk implied that the body's wisdom fails but the spirit's wisdom grows. In his schema, the seventh state (*senium*) leads to a positive fear of God and eventually to heaven. Each mature man or woman, therefore, has completed a life of grace and can now reap the greatest reward imaginable— eternal glory lived with God in heaven.[8] What more could anyone ask for?

A TIME TO SOW

There is the cliché that you can't teach an old dog new tricks, but we've just seen that keeping your intellect active and productive was regarded as an important part of remaining vital in body, mind, and soul according to the ancient world. This is a lesson the modern world is embracing. Maybe we can play with the cliché. Is it possible for an old dog to teach tricks to the young? There's no question that the answer is yes. Therefore, old age is not only a time to reap, but also a time to keep sowing. As Pope Francis expressed in a surprising and engaging way, "The elderly are also the future of a people."[9]

So at just what age could a person fairly start handing out advice and sowing wisdom? Maimonides and Petrarch told us that old age is in the eye of the beholder. You can say you're old when you want to—and it should be up to you, not someone else, to make that call. This was not always so in the ancient and medieval world. The Jewish rabbinical commentary, *Pirke Avot*, labeled forty as the age ripe for discernment (the ability to make good decisions), fifty years old as the right age to offer counsel, and sixty to qualify as an elder, although we've already seen that in many cultures the word *elder* was a loose designation and that a specific age wasn't always an automatic or even necessary entrance ticket to a council of advisers or decision makers. A medieval adoption of this commentary teaches that a man attains wisdom at forty and can give counsel once he turns fifty.[10]

Cicero offered a classic statement of old age, whatever the particular year of life, as a time to sow. He taught that if you are virtuous, every day will be a happy one. But in old age, virtues are the special fruits and good memories of a life lived well. "The crowning glory of old age is authority (*auctoritas*)," which some translations render as "influence." It's likely that what Cicero meant by his choice of the Latin word *auctoritas* is the very Roman sense of *gravitas*: weight or standing. *Auctoritas* and *gravitas* relate to the honor that comes from being able, through experience, to tell young people the truth and have them take it as advice that shouldn't be ignored. Cicero believed young people should recognize, accept, and especially honor the experience represented by old age and the advice that senior citizens sow.

Cicero's Cato, who is eighty-four, remarks that one of the joys of old age is simply to have young men sit around and listen to him. Apparently, it is even better and to the older person's honor if one of these young men goes on to glory, which would reflect well on his teacher—evidence that the young person had reaped something fruitful from the advice the old person had sown. In his case, Cato speaks to Scipio, who is thirty-five. We should recall that Cicero had set his *De senectute* a century earlier, placing it about 150 BCE. Scipio would, in 146 BCE, destroy the longtime threat to Rome posed by Carthage in North Africa. Cicero, of course, knew how those Punic Wars would end. This gives Cato even more status: there he was instructing with the wisdom of his years the young man Scipio who would crush Carthage and pave the way for Rome's dominance.[11]

We recall the practical biblical example of this transition from an active life of physically doing a task to offering advice to others in Numbers 4, which describes four groups of men charged with tending the tent that housed the Ark of the Covenant. The Levites started work when they became twenty-five, while at the age of thirty, the members of three other groups took up their tasks of packing, carrying, and setting up the tent and its furnishings. These men were members of the Kohathite, Gershonite, and Merarite clans. All were forced into retirement at fifty years old, but we imagine that they gave advice to the younger men, perhaps playing a hand in their selection and training as well. We know for certain that the Levites were permitted to act as consultants: "They may assist their brothers in the tent of meeting in carrying out their duties, but they shall perform no service" (Num 8:26). Though retired, they still served.

PASSING ON WISDOM

What's the easiest way to give advice? What is the best time to sow? It is one thing to assert that an old person has earned the right to give counsel, but quite another to have someone appreciate, let alone respect and welcome, that advice. In answer to these questions, let's examine a pair of very helpful essays, one from a pagan Roman man and the other from a medieval Christian woman, in two very different places and times, but with complementary approaches.

First, the Greek biographer and moralist Plutarch (ca. 46–122 CE), addressed this very question of the business of sowing advice in an essay titled rhetorically in the fashion of his day, "Whether an Old Man Should Engage in Public Affairs."[12] After considering the pros and cons, Plutarch decided that it was indeed the task of the old to moderate the young:

> But if for no other reason, old men should engage in
> affairs of State for the education and instruction of the

young…so the discretion of old age, when mixed in the people with boiling youth drunk with reputation and ambition, may remove that which is insane and too violent.

For Plutarch, youth is full of insanity. Once youth passes and experience takes over, the old man should not leave the public stage but remain there to mitigate young fools. While an older statesman admittedly could no longer lead men in battle, he more than compensated with the dispassion that experience brings—two things largely missing in hotheaded, ambitious young men. What old men lose in physical strength, Plutarch wrote, is nothing compared with

the advantage they possess in their caution and prudence and in the fact that they do not, borne along sometimes because of past failures and sometimes as the result of vain opinion, dash headlong upon public affairs, dragging the mob along with them in confusion like the storm-tossed sea, but manage gently and moderately the matters which arise. And that is why States when they are in difficulties or in fear yearn for the rule of the elder men;…For age does not so much diminish our power to perform inferior services as it increases our power for leading and governing.

What age brings, according to Plutarch, is an insight we've heard already from Cephalus and Seneca: losing lust and desire is a gift, not something to be lamented. Old men should be happy that they no longer race after conflict and glory because these pursuits bring "envy, jealousy, and discord." As Plutarch noted,

Some of these old age does slacken and dull, but others it quenches and cools entirely, not so much by withdrawing a man from the impulse to action as by keeping him from excessive and fiery passions, so as to bring sober and settled reasoning to bear upon his thoughts.

It was just this sober and settled reasoning that the young, striving to be popular, did not possess. This fact made Plutarch point out that, from the elderly sowers,

we do not demand deeds of hand and feet, but of counsel, foresight, and speech—not such speech as makes a roar and a clamour among the people, but that which contains good sense, prudent thought, and conservatism; and in these the hoary hair and the wrinkles that people make fun of appear as witnesses to a man's experience and strengthen him by the aid of persuasiveness and the reputation for character.

Plutarch concluded that old age is primarily a time to sow good advice; it's noble to keep serving the state this way until death. In fact, Plutarch said that it was not seemly for a man who had been vigorous and consequential in his career to settle down quietly to a country estate and retire "to be extinguished by idleness as iron is destroyed by rust." Instead, he must find something useful to do so his reputation would not tarnish or wither, "but by adding constantly something new and fresh to arouse the sense of gratitude for his previous actions and make it better and lasting." What better task to engage in than to serve the state, as much by remaining involved in details or even seemingly minor affairs as by seeing the big picture: "For it is not seasonable for an aged man even to be occupied in public offices, except in those which possess some grandeur and dignity." One such job is to act as a sort of umpire when contending parties are arguing over a specific course of action or trying to make a decision. It is here that the old, experienced man will try to moderate a debate, to cool passions and discord, and to bring a group to consensus. As noted earlier, this is precisely what Nestor was trying to do when he stepped between Achilles and Agamemnon—if only they'd listened.

Our second perspective on making old age a time to sow fruitfully comes from the Middle Ages in the person of the French author Christine de Pizan, whose advice has already guided us. She explored how older women could give counsel in such a way that it would be more likely for young women to receive the advice gratefully, to admire its value, and ultimately follow it. Plutarch had put the matter rather bluntly when he asserted, "Youth is meant to obey and old age to rule." But take that approach in any historical period and it's likely you'll be talking to the backs of young folks as they walk away from you. In contrast, in her practical handbook of proper comportment called *The Treasure of the City of Ladies* or *The Book of the Three Virtues*, dating from about 1405, de Pizan offers a chapter titled, "How Elderly Ladies Ought to Conduct Themselves toward Young Ones, and the Qualities that They Ought to Have." We drew from this section when noting de Pizan's chiding of foolish old women who don't possess the good sense they should after years of experience. We learned from her that old age does not always bring wisdom—a humbling lesson in her time and ours.

Here, we turn to de Pizan's guidance on the best way to offer advice to the young. Written when she was about forty, de Pizan tells older women that they should advise younger women charitably, not irritably, even as she dips into some of the stereotypes of old people—and in this case, old women in particular—as being bitter and nasty.

> Although we say that she ought to be wise and dignified, we do not mean, however, that she should be

snappish, bad-tempered, fault-finding or rude, hoping to make people think that those are all signs of wisdom. She ought rather to guard herself against such passions as generally come to old people, namely being wrathful, spiteful and surly.

Therefore, when an old woman has something of value to say to a young person, she must take care to go against what de Pizan regards as the expected approach: the old crone as scold. Instead, she must realize that the sound advice she has to offer can be lost if it's not given in a palatable, pleasant way. The old woman must think before she speaks:

> When she feels in an argumentative or angry mood, the wise elderly lady will temper it by means of this prudent discretion, saying to herself, "Goodness, what's the matter with you? What are you trying to do? Is this the behaviour of a sensible woman, to be upset like this? If you think these things are wrong, it is not up to you to put everything right. Calm down and do not speak so spitefully. If you could see how mean your expression looks when you are in such a fury, you would be horrified. Be more approachable and more easy-going to your people, and if you have to chastise them, reprimand them more courteously. Avoid such anger, for it displeases God, and does you no good and will not make people love you. You must be patient."

De Pizan recognized the difficulty in getting anyone to accept good advice, let alone the young who think they always know better and indeed act like the proverbial know-it-alls. The wise old woman should not play into caricatures, acting the way the young expect, for then their sound advice will fall on deaf ears. Instead, she should tap into her own experience and judgment, realizing that what she has learned is valuable for the young—but that it is just as important to offer her lessons the right way.

> She should say to herself, My Lord, but you were young once; cast your mind back to the things you got up to in those days! Would you have liked people to talk about you this way? And why are you so exercised about their affairs anyway? Consider the great trials of youth. You should take pity on them, for you have passed that way yourself.
>
> One ought to correct young people and reprove them firmly for their follies, but not, however, hate or defame them, for they are not aware of what they are doing. For this reason you will put up with them tolerantly and gently rebuke them when you have to. And if others criticize or defame them, you will excuse them out of pity, remembering the ignorance of youth, which prevents their having greater knowledge.[13]

De Pizan understood, therefore, that an older person's later years were a time to become more self-aware by reflecting on her own experiences. But she should also sow the lessons she has reaped to the next generation.

Afterword

THE RICHNESS OF
BIBLICAL WISDOM

In conclusion, we return to the fundamental biblical paradox: "Is wisdom with the aged, / and understanding in length of days?" (Job 12:12). As we said at the start, any conversation about biblical wisdom must also be a conversation about aging. And those conversations must take into account not only those who first told and heard, wrote and read these biblical stories, but those who tried to understand them in their own later cultures. While also drawing on pagan understandings of age and wisdom to enlighten our biblical lessons, we have seen that the three monotheistic faiths of Judaism, Christianity, and Islam share the heritage of some of these ancient stories, too. No one group—religious or not, monotheistic or polytheistic, ancient or modern—has a monopoly on the lessons and gifts of biblical wisdom.

In the Bible and our own lives, it would be much easier and neater to say that the older we get, the wiser we become. Indeed, we have witnessed many biblical, cultural, historical, and literary passages, indicating that the more we age, the wiser we become.

The ancient Greek historian Diodorus Siculus told us at the start of our journey that history will teach us "the wisdom of the aged"—an appealing title for a book, but a misleading one, too.

As noted, some cultures pay only lip service to honoring the elderly. Ancient Greeks and Romans gave us flowery rhetoric about honoring the elderly, but they didn't always treat their older folks very well, let alone appreciate their insights. For the Athenians, it took their archenemy, the Spartans, to teach them simply how to stand up and give an old man a seat. Homer told us that we should respect old Nestor, but the young hotheads, Achilles and Agamemnon, just waited for him to stop talking so they could pick up their fight where it left off. Isaac was fooled by Rebekah and Jacob. Even wise king Solomon essentially blew it all at the end of his life. Some of our medieval commentators were unsure as to whether we should honor the elderly just because they had lived longer than others.

We also saw that, in the Bible and other cultures of its time, elders did not always have to be older. We have met specific young, wise biblical characters like Elihu and Daniel as well as medieval bishops who seemed too youthful for their jobs. Monasteries and convents offered us monks and nuns who were considered senior even if they were younger than others. Chaucer's stories are full of old folks getting cheated, yet he also gave us an example of an old man outwitting three young and greedy drunks. Chaucer's contemporary over in France, Christine de Pizan, cautioned that an old woman could be wise and unselfish or cranky and mean.

Paradoxes have been a frequent feature on this journey of ageless wisdom. We want things to be simple, but have discovered that the lessons and gifts of biblical wisdom are more rich than they are simple. We noted the irony that understanding our own growth in wisdom should make us humble rather than arrogant. Furthermore, we should learn from our experiences but never fail to keep in mind how much we still don't know—Socrates's indispensable lesson. Time and again, we came across biblical folks who continued to advocate for others even as their own time was passing: Abraham and Moses arguing with God, for instance, or Sarah and Elizabeth passing along the very gift of life in their old age. Blessings and burdens sometimes go together; it is the wise soul who can navigate an even keel between them.

Experience also leads to a sense of self. Barzillai and Naomi, for example, knew the score—they knew who they were and where they stood. They knew what they could do as well as their limitations. Their eyes were wide open and that gave them patience, perspective, and a healthy sense of humor. Even the cantankerous Jacob, in his curious blessing to his children, can't be faulted for lying. He told the truth, even if it was uncomfortable and outright hurtful—though he likely meant his honesty to be instructive, even if it was also brutal. Wisdom is like that sometimes.

Rather than yes *or* no, the answer to the question, "Is wisdom with the aged, and understanding in length of days?" seems rather to be both yes *and* no. We can be young and wise or old and foolish. But even young fools can grow in wisdom as they age if they are open to the lessons and gifts of their experience. Our best biblical models enriched their own lives by reaping the rewards of their roles as sages. They also kept sowing the seeds of their own hard-gained knowledge, insight, and experience so that, in turn, their children and grandchildren might keep handing their insights on. Such generosity is the biblical way to pay wisdom forward.

Notes

Chapter 1: Biblical Paradoxes

1. Diodorus Siculus, *Library of History*, I.1.5.

2. For a sympathetic treatment of belief, a religious approach to the Bible, and modern methods of scriptural study, see Bart D. Ehrman, *Jesus, Interrupted: Revealing the Hidden Contradictions in the Bible (and Why We Don't Know About Them)* (San Francisco: HarperOne, 2009).

3. See Rachel Zohar Dulin, *A Crown of Glory: A Biblical View of Aging* (Mahwah, NJ: Paulist Press, 1988), esp. 4–5 and a list of verses by topic at 144–45. For a comprehensive index of passages, see J. Gordon Harris, *Biblical Perspectives on Aging: God and the Elderly* (Philadelphia: Fortress Press, 1987), 138–43. See also Stephen Sapp, *Full of Years: Aging and the Elderly in the Bible and Today* (Nashville: Abingdon Press, 1987), 72–75 on wisdom. Less systematic but more spiritually oriented is Luis Alonso Schökel, *In the Autumn of Life: Biblical Meditations on Hope for the Elderly* (Slough, England: St. Paul Publications, 1991).

4. Plato, *The Last Days of Socrates*, trans. Hugh Tredennick and Harold Tarrant (London: Penguin, 2003), 44–45 (*Apology* 21a–d).

Chapter 2: Gathering Wisdom

1. Ludwig Köhler, *Hebrew Man*, trans. Peter R. Ackroyd (London: SCM Press, 1956), 42.

2. Petrarch, *Letters of Old Age*, trans. Aldo S. Bernardo, Saul Levin, and Reta A. Bernardo, 2 vols. (Baltimore: The Johns Hopkins University Press, 1992), 1:106. Despite its title, this work is not a systematic treatise about old age, but is instead a collection of the humanist's correspondence on many subjects from his later years.

3. William M. Thackston Jr., trans., *Tales of the Prophets* (Chicago: Great Books of the Islamic World, Inc., 1997), 92.

4. Herodotus, *The Histories*, trans. Aubrey de Sélincourt, rev. John Marincola (London: Penguin Books, 2003), 94 (I.216), 180 (III.23); on Cleitarchus's reference, see Ian Worthington, ed., *Alexander the Great: A Reader* (London: Routledge, 2003), 152.

5. Thorkild Jacobsen, *The Sumerian King List* (Chicago: The University of Chicago Press, 1939), with the list itself at 69–127; on Adad-guppi, see Rivkah Harris, *Gender and Aging in Mesopotamia* (Norman, OK: University of Oklahoma Press, 2000), 89.

6. A. Malamat, "Longevity: Biblical Concepts and Some Ancient Near Eastern Parallels," *Archiv für Orientforschung* 19 (1982): 220.

7. Fumimaso Fukui, "On Perennial Youth and Longevity: A Taoist View on Health of the Elderly," in *Religion, Aging and Health: A Global Perspective*, ed. William M. Clements, (New York: The Haworth Press, 1989), 119; Michael E. Goodich, *From Birth to Old Age: The Human Life Cycle in Medieval Thought, 1250–1350* (Lanham, MD: University Press of America, 1989), 153–54; William Hazlitt, trans., *The Table-Talk of Martin Luther* (London: George Bell & Sons, 1884), 65, no. 160.

8. Frank N. Egerton, III, "The Longevity of the Patriarchs: A Topic in the History of Demography," *Journal of the History of Ideas* 27 (1966): 578–80.

9. The Holy Qur'an, translated by Abdullah Yusuf Ali. First edition in 1934. See http://wikiislam.net/wiki/The_Holy_Qur%27an:_Al-Isra_(The_Night_Journey).

10. Harold M. Stahmer, "The Aged in Two Ancient Oral Cultures: The Ancient Hebrews and Homeric Greece," in *Aging and the Elderly: Humanistic Perspectives in Gerontology*, ed. Stuart F. Spicker et al. (Atlantic Highlands, NJ: Humanities Press, Inc., 1978), 31, 34–35; Shulamith Shahar, *Growing Old in the Middle Ages*, trans. Yael Lotan (London: Routledge, 1997), 88–97; Michael Signer, "Honour the Hoary Head: The Aged in the Medieval European Jewish Community," in *Aging and the Aged in Medieval Europe*, ed. Michael M. Sheehan (Toronto: Pontifical Institute of Mediaeval Studies, 1990), 39–48; Tim Parkin, "The Ancient Greek and Roman Worlds," in *A History of Old Age*, ed. Pat Thane (Los Angeles: J. Paul Getty Museum, 2005), 44–45. On the Ojibway, see John A. Grim, "Aging among Native Americans: The Quest for Wisdom," in *Aging: Spiritual Perspectives*, ed. Francis V. Tiso (Lake Worth, FL: Sunday Publications, Inc., 1982), 29. For the Qur'an reference, see Stephen Sapp, "Aging in World Religions: An Overview," in *A Guide to Humanistic Studies in Aging: What Does It Mean to Grow Old?* ed. Thomas R. Cole, Ruth E. Ray, and Robert Kastenbaum (Baltimore: The Johns Hopkins University Press, 2010), 134–35.

11. Moshe Weinfeld, "The Phases of Human Life in Mesopotamian and Jewish Sources," in *Priests, Prophets and Scribes*, ed. Eugene Ulrich et al. (Sheffield: JSOT/Sheffield Academic Press, 1992), 182–83; Robert L. Katz, "Jewish Values and Sociopsychological Perspectives on Aging," *Pastoral Psychology* 24 (1975): 139 (*Ethics of the Fathers* 5:21).

12. J. A. Burrow, *The Ages of Man: A Study in Medieval Thought and Writing* (Oxford: Clarendon Press, 1986), 191–202; Tim G. Parkin, *Old Age in the Roman World: A Cultural and Social History* (Baltimore: The Johns Hopkins University Press, 2003), 279; Sapp, "Aging in World Religions: An Overview," 124, 136–37n4; Luke Demaitre, "The Care and Extension of Old Age in Medieval Medicine," in *Aging and the Aged in Medieval Europe*, 8; Goodich, *From Birth to Old Age*, 62–63. For the most comprehensive treatment of the subject, with many helpful illustrations, exceptionally informative and helpful is Elizabeth Sears, *The Ages of Man: Medieval Interpretations of the Life Cycle* (Princeton: Princeton University Press, 1986).

13. *Rashi's Commentary on Psalms*, trans. Mayer I. Gruber (Leiden: Brill, 2004), 425; Arthur Waley, trans., *The Analects of Confucius* (New York: Vintage Books, 1938), II.4, 88.

14. Reuven Hammer, trans., *The Classic Midrash: Tannaitic Commentaries on the Bible* (New York: Paulist Press, 1995), 391–92.

15. Kofi Appiah-Kubi, "Knowledge Is Power, but Age Is Wisdom: The Challenge of Active Aging from an African Perspective," in *Aging: Spiritual Perspectives*, ed. Francis V. Tiso, (Lake Worth, FL: Sunday Publications, Inc., 1982), 22.

16. Plato, *Laws*, 931d; Albert Chi-Lu Chung, "The Elderly and Moral Precepts in Chinese Tradition," in *Aging: Spiritual Perspectives*, 51–55; Patricia Buckley Ebrey, ed., *Chinese Civilization: A Sourcebook*, 2nd ed. (New York: The Free Press, 1993), 66 (*Classic of Filial Piety*, 10); Sapp, "Aging in World Religions," 132–33; Walpola Rahula, *What the Buddha Taught*, rev. ed. (New York: Grove Press, 1974), 78–79.

17. Plato, *Laws*, 879c, 880a.

18. Hesiod, *Theogony*, ll. 21–25. For classic and recent summaries of ancient examples, see Bessie Ellen Richardson, *Old Age among the Ancient Greeks* (Baltimore: The Johns Hopkins

University Press, 1933), esp. 1–30, and Thomas M. Falkner, *The Poetics of Old Age in Greek Epic, Lyric, and Tragedy* (Norman: University of Oklahoma Press, 1995).

19. Homer, *The Iliad*, trans. Robert Fagles (New York: Penguin, 1990), 85–87 (I.290–364).

Chapter 3: Being Wise, Being Humble

1. George R. Coffman, "Old Age from Horace to Chaucer: Some Literary Affinities and Adventures of an Idea," *Speculum: A Journal of Medieval Studies* 9 (1934): 269–77; Alicia K. Nitecki, "The Convention of the Old Man's Lament in the *Pardoner's Tale*," *The Chaucer Review* 16 (1981–82): 76–84.

2. Rivkah Harris, *Gender and Aging in Mesopotamia* (Norman, OK: University of Oklahoma Press, 2000), 50–51, 91, 100–107; Michael A. Signer, "Honour the Hoary Head: The Aged in the Medieval European Jewish Community," in *Aging and the Aged in Medieval Europe*, ed. Michael M. Sheehan (Toronto: Pontifical Institute of Mediaeval Studies, 1990), 41–44.

3. David Philipson, www.JewishEncyclopedia.com, s.v. "Age, Old."

4. J. Gordon Harris, *Biblical Perspectives on Aging: God and the Elderly* (Philadelphia: Fortress Press 1987), 98; and Philipson, s.v. "Age, Old."

5. Georges Minois, *History of Old Age from Antiquity to the Renaissance*, trans. Sarah Hanbury Tenison (Chicago: The University of Chicago Press, 1989), 117–18.

6. Much of what follows is informed by Hanoch Reviv, *The Elders in Ancient Israel*, trans. Lucy Plitmann (Jerusalem: The Magnes Press, 1989); and A. E. Harvey, "Elders," *Journal of Theological Studies* 25 (1974): 318–32.

7. Cyril C. Richardson, trans., *Early Christian Fathers* (New York: Touchstone, 1996), Ignatius's *Letter to the Magnesians*, 95 (3.1).

8. Owen Chadwick, trans., *Western Asceticism* (Philadelphia: The Westminster Press, 1958), 296–97 (*Regula*, chap. 3), 331–32 (*Regula*, chaps. 63–64). Notice that Benedict himself drew on an example of biblical wisdom in order to make his point.

9. Chadwick, trans., *Western Asceticism*, 331–32 (*Regula*, chaps. 63–64). On the inconsistent use of the phrases and what they meant, see Giles Constable, "*Seniores* et *pueri* à Cluny aux Xe, XIe siècles," in *Histoire et société: Mélanges offerts à Georges Duby*, 17–24 (Aix-en-Provence: Université de Provence, 1992), reprinted in Giles Constable, *Cluny from the Tenth to the Twelfth Centuries: Further Studies* (Aldershot: Ashgate Variorum, 2000), selection II. For the Buddhist monastic custom, see Daw Khin Myo Chit, "Add Life to Years the Buddhist Way," in *Religion, Aging and Health: A Global Perspective*, ed. William M. Clements (New York: The Haworth Press, 1989), 41.

10. Minois, *History of Old Age from Antiquity*, 118–19.

11. Ben Zion Bokser, trans., *The Talmud: Selected Writings* (New York: Paulist Press, 1989), 231, citing *Ethics of the Fathers* 1:26; Harris, *Biblical Perspectives on Aging*, 99, citing *Ethics of the Fathers* 4:25–27. See also Robert L. Katz, "Jewish Values and Sociopsychological Perspectives on Aging," *Pastoral Psychology* 24 (1975): 137, citing a similar passage in *Ethics of the Fathers* 4:20.

12. Philipson, s.v. "Age, Old."

13. For the first translation, see Rashi, *Commentaries on the Pentateuch*, trans. Chaim Pearl (New York: W.W. Norton & Company, Inc., 1970), 127. For the second translation, see Rashi, *Commentary on the Torah*, vol. 3, *Vayikra/Leviticus*, trans. Yisrael Isser Zvi Herczeg et al. (Brooklyn: Mesorah Publications, 1994), 247, and nn. 1–2 for Rashi's indication of what makes a condemnable elder ignorant.

14. Arthur Waley, trans., *The Analects of Confucius* (New York: Vintage Books, 1938), 88 (XIV.46); Stephen Sapp, "Aging in World Religions: An Overview," in *A Guide to Humanistic Studies in Aging: What Does It Mean to Grow Old?* eds. Thomas R. Cole, Ruth E. Ray, and Robert Kastenbaum (Baltimore: The Johns Hopkins University Press, 2010), 133 (*Dhammapada* 19.260–61).

15. Christine de Pizan, *The Treasure of the City of Ladies* or *The Book of the Three Virtues*, trans. Sarah Lawson (Harmondsworth: Penguin, 2003), 147, 151–52.

16. Philipson, s.v. "Age, Old." It's interesting to note that a long-term study of adult development that tracked over eight hundred people for more than fifty years concluded that wisdom does not necessarily increase with age, finding that most folks thought middle age had been their wisest period. The author determined that a chapter titled, "Does Wisdom Increase with Age?" was best described as "this ambiguous chapter": George E. Vaillant, *Aging Well: Surprising Guideposts to a Happier Life from the Landmark Harvard Study of Adult Development* (Boston: Little, Brown and Company, 2002), 249–56.

Chapter 4: Let's Make a Deal, God

1. William M. Brinner, trans., *Lives of the Prophets* (Leiden: Brill, 2002), 164–65. For variations, see John Renard, *Friends of God: Islamic Images of Piety, Commitment, and Servanthood* (Berkeley: University of California Press, 2008), 131; and William M. Thackston Jr., trans., *Tales of the Prophets* (Chicago: Great Books of the Islamic World, Inc., 1997), 162–63.

2. A delightful exploration of this kind of bargaining is Michael Wex, *Born to Kvetch: Yiddish Language and Culture in All Its Moods* (New York: St. Martin's Press, 2005). It is best enjoyed as an audio book read by the author to get his inflections

and other subtleties of spoken language; it is more instructive, in fact, to hear this book than simply to read it.

3. Here we are reminded of the sixteenth-century saint Teresa of Ávila: thrown from her horse into a muddy puddle, she declared wryly to God, "If this is how you treat your friends, no wonder you have so few."

4. Reuven Hammer, trans., *The Classic Midrash: Tannaitic Commentaries on the Bible* (New York: Paulist Press, 1995), 277.

5. We find this deathbed scene related by several Greco-Roman historians; see, for instance, Ian Worthington, ed., *Alexander the Great: A Reader* (London: Routledge, 2003), 5.

6. Moshe Ch. Sosevsky, trans., *Samuel II: A New English Translation*, ed. A. J. Rosenberg (New York: Judaica Press, 1992), 394–95.

7. Plato, *Republic*, trans. R. E. Allen (New Haven: Yale University Press, 2006), 2–6 (328B–331D).

Chapter 5: Blessings and Burdens

1. J. Gordon Harris, *Biblical Perspectives on Aging: God and the Elderly* (Philadelphia: Fortress Press, 1987), 21; A. Malamat, "Longevity: Biblical Concepts and Some Ancient Near Eastern Parallels," *Archiv für Orientforschung* 19 (1982): 219.

2. Rashi, *Commentary on the Torah*, vol. 2, *Shemos/Exodus*, trans. Yisrael Isser Zvi Herczeg et al. (Brooklyn: Mesorah Publications, 1994), 239; Malamat, "Longevity," 219; Harris, *Biblical Perspectives on Aging*, 20.

3. Cicero, *De senectute, De amicitia, De divinatione*, trans. William Armistead Falconer (Cambridge: Harvard University Press, 1923), 75–77 (*De senectute*, XVIII.63–64).

4. Christine de Pizan, *The Treasure of the City of Ladies* or *The Book of the Three Virtues*, trans. Sarah Lawson (Harmondsworth: Penguin, 2003), 150–51.

5. For a survey of opinions on the issue of quantity and quality of long life, see "Living to 120 and Beyond: Americans' Views on Aging, Medical Advances and Radical Life Extension," Pew Research Center's Religion and Public Life Project, 2013.

6. Rashi, *Commentary on the Torah*, vol. 2, *Shemos/Exodus*, 373–74. See also Harris, *Biblical Perspectives on Aging*, 14; and Hans Walter Wolff, "Problems between the Generations in the Old Testament," in *Essays in Old Testament Ethics*, ed. James L. Crenshaw and John T. Willis (New York: KTAV, 1974), 81–82.

7. Plato, *Laws*, II.924c.

8. Nadine Bernard, "Les femmes âgées au sein de la famille et de la cité classique," in *L'ancienneté chez les anciens*, vol. 1, *La vieillesse dans les sociétés antiques: La Grèce et Rome*, ed. Béatrice Bakhouche (Montpellier: Université Paul-Valéry Montpellier III, 2003), 56–60.

9. Rashi, *Samuel I: A New English Translation of the Text and Rashi, with a Commentary Digest*, ed. and trans. A. J. Rosenberg (New York: Judaica Press, 1991), 61, 86–87.

10. Rashi, *Commentary on the Torah*, vol. 4, *Bamidbar/Numbers*, trans. Yisrael Isser Zvi Herczeg et al. (Brooklyn: Mesorah Publications, 1997), 4.

11. Cicero, *De senectute, De amicitia, De divinatione*, 17 (*De senectute*, III.8), 23 (*De senectute*, V.14), 39 (*De senectute*, IX.30); Tim G. Parkin, *Old Age in the Roman World: A Cultural and Social History* (Baltimore: The Johns Hopkins University Press, 2003), 1–12, 239–76.

12. Lothario dei Segni, *On the Misery of the Human Condition: De miseria humane conditionis*, trans. Margaret Mary Dietz (Indianapolis: Bobbs-Merrill, 1969), 13 (I.X). For a reconsideration of the traditional interpretation of this text, see John C. Moore, "Innocent III's *De Miseria Humanae Conditionis: A Speculum Curiae?*" *Catholic Historical Review* 67 (1981): 553–64.

Chapter 6: Patience and Humor

1. Rashi, *Commentary on the Torah*, vol. 1, *Bereishis/Genesis*, trans. Yisrael Isser Zvi Herczeg et al. (Brooklyn: Mesorah Publications, 1995), 242, 267.

2. Jacobus de Voragine, *The Golden Legend: Readings on the Saints*, trans. William Granger Ryan, 2 vols. (Princeton: Princeton University Press, 1993), 1:330.

3. Vatican Radio transcript, February 2, 2014.

4. Martin Luther, *The Sermons of Martin Luther* (Grand Rapids, MI: Baker Book House, 1983), 1:257–307. We should note that this is a harsh, painfully over-interpreted sermon that readers will find insulting to Jews and Catholics.

5. P. M. Matarasso, trans., *Quest of the Holy Grail* (Harmondsworth: Penguin, 1969), 103–8, with quotation at p. 107. There are many legends about the Holy Grail, of course, and another has a link, albeit slightly broken, with this story, too. In this other widespread version, a character referred to as the Fisher King or the Maimed King had been wounded by the lance of Longinus, the Roman centurion who thrust his spear into Jesus' side on the cross. This king, who seems affiliated with the wounded Mordrain, is injured in his groin or thigh, perhaps a reference to sexual sterility or impotence or a way to explain that he cannot walk. The Fisher or Maimed King is the keeper of the grail, but in this rendering he is a direct descendant of Joseph of Arimathea, which doesn't quite fit Perceval's story, where Mordrain is not a blood relative of Joseph, although he has protected Josephus, his son. Fans of the movies *Monty Python and the Holy Grail* (1975) or *Indiana Jones and the Last Crusade* (1989) will recognize modern-day retellings and appropriations of these ancient and medieval stories.

6. Shulamith Shahar, *Growing Old in the Middle Ages*, trans. Yael Lotan (London: Routledge, 1997), 13.

7. Petrarch, *Letters of Old Age*, trans. Aldo S. Bernardo, Saul Levin, and Reta A. Bernardo, 2 vols. (Baltimore: The Johns Hopkins University Press, 1992), 1:263–69, with quotation at 265.

8. Pew Research Center Publications, "Growing Old in America: Expectations vs. Reality," released June 29, 2009, www.pewresearch.org; *New York Times*, June 30, 2009.

Chapter 7: A Time to Reap, A Time to Sow

1. Homer, *The Iliad*, trans. Robert Fagles (New York: Penguin, 1990), 204 (VI.318–29).

2. Nadine Bernard, "Les femmes âgées au sein de la famille et de la cité classique," in *L'ancienneté chez les anciens*, vol. 1, *La vieillesse dans les sociétés antiques: La Grèce et Rome*, ed. Béatrice Bakhouche (Montpellier: Université Paul-Valéry Montpellier III, 2003), 53–55; Tim G. Parkin, *Old Age in the Roman World: A Cultural and Social History* (Baltimore: The Johns Hopkins University Press, 2003), 259n102 (Plato, *Laws*, 6.759d; Aristotle, *Politics* 7.1329a).

3. Andrew George, trans., *The Epic of Gilgamesh* (London: Penguin, 1999), *Tablet* XI.

4. Rivkah Harris, *Gender and Aging in Mesopotamia* (Norman, OK: University of Oklahoma Press, 2000), 31, 51–52.

5. Cicero, *De senectute, De amicitia, De divinatione*, trans. William Armistead Falconer (Cambridge: Harvard University Press, 1923), 29–35 (*De senectute*, VII.21–VIII.26).

6. Seneca. *Letters from a Stoic*, trans. Robin Campbell (Harmondsworth: Penguin, 1969), 58 (*Letter* XII).

7. Quoted by Karen Cokayne, *Experiencing Old Age in Ancient Rome* (London: Routledge, 2003), 93.

8. Elizabeth Sears, *The Ages of Man: Medieval Interpretations of the Life Cycle* (Princeton: Princeton University Press, 1986), 128–29, 198–99n42.

9. *The New York Times*, July 22, 2013.

10. Robert L. Katz, "Jewish Values and Sociopsychological Perspectives on Aging," *Pastoral Psychology* 24 (1975): 139 (*Ethics of the Fathers* 5:21); Michael E. Goodich, *From Birth to Old Age: The Human Life Cycle in Medieval Thought, 1250–1350* (Lanham, MD: University Press of America, 1989), 62.

11. Cicero, *De senectute, De amicitia, De divinatione*, 13, 17–18 (*De senectute*, II.4, 9); for *apex est autem senectutis auctoritas*, see 73 (*De senectute*, XVII.61); 27 (*De senectute*, VI.17); 39–41 (*De senectute*, X.31).

12. Plutarch, *Moralia*, vol. X, trans. Harold North Fowler (Cambridge, MA: Harvard University Press, 1960), 77–153 (*Moralia* 783B–797F).

13. Christine de Pizan, *The Treasure of the City of Ladies* or *The Book of the Three Virtues*, trans. Sarah Lawson (Harmondsworth: Penguin, 2003), 148–49.

Select Bibliography

Readers interested in exploring particular points may find specific sources in the endnotes. What I have offered here is a very general bibliography confined largely to books.

Burrow, J. A. *The Ages of Man: A Study in Medieval Thought and Writing*. Oxford: Clarendon Press, 1986.

Chittister, Joan. *The Gift of Years: Growing Older Gracefully*. New York: BlueBridge, 2008.

Clements, William M., ed. *Ministry with the Aging*. New York: The Haworth Press, 1989.

Cole, Thomas R., and Mary G. Winkler, eds. *The Oxford Book of Aging: Reflections on the Journey of Life*. Oxford: Oxford University Press, 1994.

Cole, Thomas R. et al., eds. *A Guide to Humanistic Studies in Aging: What Does It Mean to Grow Old?* Baltimore, MD: Johns Hopkins University Press, 2010.

Crenshaw, James L. *Old Testament Wisdom: An Introduction*. Louisville, KY: Westminster John Knox Press, 1998.

Dulin, Rachel Zohar. *A Crown of Glory: A Biblical View of Aging*. Mahwah, NJ: Paulist Press, 1988.

Egerton III, Frank N. "The Longevity of the Patriarchs: A Topic in the History of Demography." *Journal of the History of Ideas* 27 (1966): 575–84.

Fowler, James W. *Stages of Faith: The Psychology of Human Development and the Quest for Meaning.* San Francisco: Harper & Row, 1981.

Goodich, Michael E. *From Birth to Old Age: The Human Life Cycle in Medieval Thought, 1250-1350.* Lanham, MD: University Press of America, 1989.

Harris, J. Gordon. *Biblical Perspectives on Aging: God and the Elderly.* Philadelphia: Fortress Press, 1987.

Harris, Rivkah. *Gender and Aging in Mesopotamia.* Norman, OK: University of Oklahoma Press, 2000.

Harvey, A. E. "Elders." *Journal of Theological Studies* 25 (1974): 318–32.

Malamat, A. "Longevity: Biblical Concepts and Some Ancient Near Eastern Parallels." *Archiv für Orientforschung* 19 (1982): 215–24.

Minois, Georges. *History of Old Age from Antiquity to the Renaissance.* Translated by Sarah Hanbury Tenison. Chicago: The University of Chicago Press, 1989.

Pilch, John J. *Introducing the Cultural Context of the Old Testament.* Mahwah, NJ: Paulist Press, 1991.

Pilch, John J., and Bruce J. Malina, eds. *Handbook of Biblical Social Values.* Peabody, MA: Hendrickson Publishers, 1998.

Reviv, Hanoch. *The Elders in Ancient Israel.* Translated by Lucy Plitmann. Jerusalem: The Magnes Press, 1989.

Sapp, Stephen. *Full of Years: Aging and the Elderly in the Bible and Today.* Nashville: Abingdon Press, 1987.

Schökel, Luis Alonso. *In the Autumn of Life: Biblical Meditations on Hope for the Elderly.* Slough, England: St. Paul Publications, 1991.

Sears, Elizabeth. *The Ages of Man: Medieval Interpretations of the Life Cycle*. Princeton: Princeton University Press, 1986.

Shahar, Shulamith. *Growing Old in the Middle Ages*. Translated by Yael Lotan. London: Routledge, 1997.

Sheehan, Michael M., ed. *Aging and the Aged in Medieval Europe*. Toronto: Pontifical Institute of Mediaeval Studies, 1990.

Telushkin, Joseph. *Jewish Wisdom: Ethical, Spiritual, and Historical Lessons from the Great Works and Thinkers*. New York: William Morrow and Company, Inc., 1994.

Thane, Pat, ed. *A History of Old Age*. Los Angeles: J. Paul Getty Museum, 2005.

Vaillant, George E. *Aging Well: Surprising Guideposts to a Happier Life from the Landmark Harvard Study of Adult Development*. Boston: Little, Brown and Company, 2002.

Vaux, Roland de. *Ancient Israel: Its Life and Institutions*. Grand Rapids, MI: Eerdmans, 1997.

Youngs, Deborah. *The Life Cycle in Western Europe, c.1300–c.1500*. Manchester: Manchester University Press, 2006.